TOWN of HANOVER

1761-2011

*A collection of essays and photographs celebrating
the 250th anniversary of
the Town of Hanover, New Hampshire*

Jon Gilbert Fox

Hanover Improvement Society

2011

Hanover, New Hampshire   1761-2011

© 2011 by the Hanover Improvement Society, Hanover, New Hampshire USA

ISBN 978-1-4276-5178-5
Library of Congress Control Number: 2011906062

For all general information, please contact:
Hanover Improvement Society
57 South Main Street, PO Box 106
Hanover, NH 03755
Telephone: (603) 643-2408

The Book Committee
Marilyn (Willy) Black
Thomas Byrne
Jack DeGange, Editor

Production
Book Design: Dana Flewelling, Sutton, NH
Index: Christine Hoskin, Etna, NH
Logo Design: Lori Prior, Lebanon, NH
Printing: Whitman Communications, Lebanon, NH
Photography: Principal color photography by Jon Gilbert Fox. Historic photography primarily from the collection of Frank J. Barrett, Jr., and the Dartmouth College Library. Selected Dartmouth College views by Joseph Mehling. Additional photography from various sources with credit where appropriate.

Cover illustration (front, back): Commemorative logo by Lori Prior. Original charter (front and reverse) courtesy of Dartmouth College Library.

Acknowledgment

It is impossible to thank by name the great number of citizens and organizations that have assisted in this book's development. It is truly a community project that reflects the generous spirit of the Town of Hanover, New Hampshire.

Jon Gilbert Fox

Members of the Hanover 250 Book Committee include, seated: Marilyn (Willy) Black and Tom Byrne. Standing: Jack DeGange

Foreword

In 2007, when this book was little more than a vague promise, Marilyn (Willy) Black and Tom Byrne, the driving forces in its evolution as a part of the celebration of Hanover's 250th celebration, met with Edward Connery Lathem.

Edward Connery Lathem

Joseph Mehling

Mr. Lathem, dean of libraries emeritus of Dartmouth College and a noted author and editor, was chairman of the Hanover Bicentennial Committee, and a principal contributor with Francis Lane Childs, an English professor at Dartmouth, to the bicentennial book published in 1961.

Professor Childs was the editor of that book. With 22 chapters written by 21 members of the Hanover community (Professor Childs wrote two chapters), the book's 275 pages included only 47 historic photographs. It was a product of its time.

Mr. Lathem recognized that a similar approach to the 250th anniversary book wouldn't satisfy the tastes and expectations of readers in 2011. In simplest terms he advised, "Be visual." Unfortunately, Mr. Lathem died in 2009. The Book Committee has strived to remain faithful to his vision: Fewer words, more photos.

This book presents articles and photographs that are representative of the Town of Hanover's history during the past 50 years. Readers are invited to start at the beginning, somewhere in the middle, or the end. The content isn't dissimilar to the bicentennial book (available at Howe Library) that can also be entered wherever the reader's interest leads.

While this book addresses the period from 1961 to the present, there is a timeline that includes notable events dating from Hanover's beginning in 1761. Also provided is a list of suggested books that are ample reference for those in search of more about the history of the Town and the College.

Rather than 21 contributors, as was the case in 1961, in 2011 the Book Committee has invited nearly 50 members of the community, past and present, to share their recollections. Call it history in the words of those who have lived it.

In the afterword of the bicentennial book, Mr. Lathem, a distinguished man of letters, wrote, "If the present is at all to insinuate itself into the future, such interjection ought, probably, to be in terms of broadly stated hopes, rather than specific expectations or prophecy. Accordingly, perhaps 1961 in looking onward into Hanover's third century may simply record a general wish for the years ahead: that this historic town may always be for all its citizens a pleasant, an interesting, and a rewarding community, whatever the character of its society or the nature of its institutions at any given time."

In 2011, half way through Hanover's third century, that wish is unwavering. *(J.D.)*

The Hanover Improvement Society

Among its numerous contributions to the Town of Hanover, the Hanover Improvement Society (HIS) has donated the funds to produce this book and to serve as publisher. On behalf of all who will enjoy this pictorial review of Hanover's history during the past 50 years, the Book Committee gratefully acknowledges the Society's unfailing generosity.

On more than one occasion, Lou Bressett called the Improvement Society "Hanover's Fairy Godmother." Since 1922, and especially through the millions of dollars it has contributed to the betterment of the Town since 1961, the Society has added much to the quality of life of Hanover citizens.

The roots of the HIS can be traced to the Ornamental Tree Association founded in 1874 by Hiram Hitchcock and others. Their mission was to enhance the "desirableness of our Village" with shade trees.

In 1892, the renamed Hanover Tree Association's mission was expanded to include the improvement of streets, sidewalks, walks, parks and the village common, all designed to "promote the growth and prosperity" of the village.

In 1922, Frank F. and Frank W. Davison, owners of the successful Nugget Theater (opened in 1916) offered to donate the thriving business to the Town with the condition that all net proceeds "be used for the benefit of the Town." Since state law prohibited the town from operating any business that might lose money, town leaders formed the not-for-profit Hanover Improvement Society.

The original officers of the self-perpetuating Society were the three precinct commissioners and 17 other citizens including Dartmouth's president, Ernest Martin Hopkins, and Adna (Dave) Storrs, a descendant of an early settler in the town.

In practice, a partnership developed among the Society, downtown businesses, Dartmouth College, and town government. The Society's approach to its work was, quietly and without fanfare, to do what needed to be done.

The main business of HIS was to run the Nugget Theater profitably to generate funds for public works and community improvements. In 1935, during the latter years of the depression, the mission changed as federal funds led to the development of the Storrs Pond Recreation Area.

The Storrs Pond Recreation area: a community resource for decades.

In 1951, the Nugget moved from West Wheelock Street to South Main Street. In 1970, the Nugget Arcade was built adjacent to the theater. It became home to HIS offices with other space leased for commercial uses. The Nugget has evolved from a single 900-seat theater to two theaters (1975) and four in 1997.

In the 1960s and 70s, HIS resources were used to develop recreation fields, tennis courts and the swimming pool at Storrs Pond. In the late 1980s, HIS teamed with parents and friends of the Hanover youth hockey program to build the James Campion III Hockey Rink on Route 10, south of Hanover.

During the past 20 years, the Society has worked closely with town government to refurbish and modernize Main Street with light poles, trees and tree grates,

The James Campion III Rink

benches, and granite curbing and bollards. HIS also collaborated with the Hanover Garden Club to develop an array of attractive seasonal flower gardens that welcome visitors and adorn Main Street.

Hundreds of smaller projects have received HIS support including skiing at Oak Hill, caring for Occom Pond, playgrounds and mini-parks around town, Costello Field in Etna, and welcoming signage for the town. The Society has also been a major contributor to the construction of the municipal parking garage, the Richard Black Community Center and to the construction (and subsequent expansion) of Howe Library.

Today, the Society has a membership of 26 community leaders, a general manager and a seven-person board of directors. Its good work is ongoing.

Improvement Society Leadership

HIS has had seven presidents since 1922: Adna (Dave) Storrs, 1922-49; Edward (Pete) Cavaney, 1949-73; Lewis (Lou) Bressett, 1973-91; John (Jack) Skewes 1991-99; Tod Schweizer, 1999-2004; John Hochreiter, 2004-10, and Randall Mudge, since 2010.

Two other community leaders deserve mention for their roles with HIS. Max Norton, a financial officer at Dartmouth for many years, was clerk and treasurer of the Society from 1930-72 and a director from 1930-86. Jack Stebbins, a Hanover attorney, was a director for 50 years prior to his death in 1997 and successor to Norton as the Society's clerk from 1972-91. *(T.B.)*

The Improvement Society's leadership in the 1970s reflected community leadership. Seated: Lou Bressett and Paul Young. Standing, from left: Roger Ball, Clint Fuller, Dick Fowler, Jack Skewes, Jack Stebbins and Dave Bradley.

So, What To Call It?

Some historic celebrations are easy to define: A centennial is 100 years, a sesquicentennial is 150 years, a bicentennial is 200 years, a tercentennial (some would say tercentenary) is 300 years and a quincentennial is 500 years.

But, when it comes to a celebration of 250 years, there are options that are good candidates for a spelling bee. Plus, it helps if you studied Latin. Consider these:

Some local historians prefer quartermillenial or semiquincentennial (probably a modern coined word).

Princeton University (1996) and Washington and Lee University (1999) used bicenquinquagenary. It's also a favorite for some other towns in New Hampshire and Vermont that join Hanover in celebrating the granting of charters by Benning Wentworth, the provincial governor, in 1761.

So, choose your choice. In the meantime, the committee producing this book decided to keep it simple: Happy 250th, Hanover!

Reference Books

For additional facts and details on the history of Hanover and Dartmouth College, readers are referred to:

Chase, Frederick (John K. Lord, editor). A History of Dartmouth College and the Town of Hanover (to 1815). Cambridge, University Press, 1891. (Second edition published in 1928.)

Lord, John K. A History of Dartmouth College, 1815-1909. Concord, Rumford Press, 1913.

Richardson, Leon Burr. A History of Dartmouth College (2 Volumes). Hanover, Dartmouth Press, 1932.

Hill, Ralph N., editor. The College on the Hill; A Dartmouth Chronicle. Hanover, Dartmouth Publications, 1964.

Graham, Robert B. The Dartmouth Story; A Narrative History of the College Buildings, People, and Legends. Hanover, Dartmouth Bookstore, Inc., 1990.

Childs, Francis L., editor. Hanover, New Hampshire, a Bicentennial Book, 1961, Town of Hanover, N.H., Vermont Printing Company, 1961.

Barrett, Frank J., Jr. Hanover, New Hampshire. Arcadia Publishing (Images of America Series), 1997, 2000.

Barrett, Frank J., Jr. Hanover, New Hampshire (Volume II). Arcadia Publishing (Images of America Series), 1998.

Barrett, Frank J., Jr. Early Dartmouth College and Downtown Hanover. Arcadia Publishing (Images of America Series), 2008.

Meacham, Scott. Dartmouth College, An Architectural Tour. Princeton Architectural Press, 2008.

Contents

The Village at the College

How "small town" was Hanover, New Hampshire as it approached its bicentennial in 1961?

There were no traffic lights in the village.

Direct dial telephone service was still on the horizon. The phone company operators had a bird's eye view of Main Street from their second floor location just down from the Hanover Inn. One day an operator told a caller she wouldn't complete his call because, "I just saw your party walking into the bookstore."

Raw sewage flowed directly into the Connecticut River.

There were still 27 working farms. Barely a decade later, they would be gone.

Banking was transacted in the imposing building shared by Dartmouth National and Dartmouth Savings.

It wasn't until 1963 that the U.S. Postal Service made "03755" a requirement for mail delivery to Hanover (Etna became 03750).

If visitors to town didn't stay at the Hanover Inn, the next-best option was the Chieftain Motel on Lyme Road.

Through its first 200 years, after Provincial Governor Benning Wentworth's royal charter established it on July 4, 1761, Hanover was a bucolic village nestled against the Connecticut River. Central to the town's history was Dartmouth College, growing to be recognized nationally for educating men (now women, too) and turning out good football teams.

Main Street, extending north through the college campus, offered modest retail commerce. Beyond the precinct district, over Balch Hill and Velvet Rocks to Etna and Hanover Center, the town was like virtually all other towns in central and northern New Hampshire: a patchwork quilt of farms.

When President Dwight D. Eisenhower visited on a beautiful June weekend in 1953 for Dartmouth's commencement, he said, "This is what a college ought to look like." His perspective easily could be extended to include the "Village at the College."

Change in Hanover was negligible as it celebrated its bicentennial but, like the rest of the nation during the years following World War II, times were changing. As the 1960s unfolded, a number of significant events evolved that would define the history of Hanover and the surrounding communities that comprise the Upper Valley region east and west of the Connecticut River, adding the word "micropolitan" to the vocabulary.

In roughly chronological order, here's what happened:

• In 1962, the opening of The Hopkins Center, a dramatic departure from Dartmouth's traditional architecture, established the College—and Hanover—as a regional year-round center for the arts and culture.

• The consolidation of Hanover's governing process in 1963 brought the village precinct and the Town's outlying areas closer together in addressing the community's collective needs.

• The creation, also in 1963, of the Dresden School District, the nation's first two-state public school district, brought students from Hanover and Norwich, Vermont together in a coordinated learning environment.

• During the late 60s, the interstate highway system reached the Upper Valley: I-89, reaching from Concord through Lebanon and beyond into Vermont, simplified access to Boston and points beyond in Vermont. I-91, on the Vermont side of the river, improved the north-south transit from Connecticut to Canada and led to the death of passenger traffic by rail.

• Dartmouth's role in the evolution of computer technology in the 1960s has influenced the way we live, work, learn and play.

• The advent of coeducation and year-round operation at Dartmouth in 1972 changed the College's undergraduate profile from about 3,000 men to, in time, over 4,000 women and men in virtually equal numbers. The year-round academic calendar, just as The Hopkins Center had done a decade earlier, led to growth and change in Main Street's commercial profile.

• The growth of the Dartmouth-Hitchcock Medical Center—Mary Hitchcock Memorial Hospital, the Hitchcock Clinic, and Dartmouth Medical School—through the 1970s and 80s has had an immeasurable influence on Hanover and the region. DHMC's relocation from Hanover to its new campus in Lebanon in 1991, and the Center's place as one of New Hampshire's largest employers, ranks as perhaps the region's most significant event in the past half-century.

These events are distinctive in Hanover's recent history. They're the most obvious changes. There are other factors as well that help to define Hanover in 2011. Some make the town different while also providing a comforting sameness.

If Dartmouth made Hanover a company town for decades, the College, now a research university in everything but name, and the relocation of the Medical Center to Lebanon, have fostered demographic changes and created the need for greater multi-community cooperation in what is now a company region.

Residential expansion, including condominiums and retirement communities, has evolved throughout Hanover over the past 40 years. Slowly, the town's population has grown by about one-third since 1960 to nearly 11,000 (counting Dartmouth students), raising the need for compact and affordable housing. Parking and traffic have been concerns for years—the numbers are bigger today. Some things defy solution despite the energy and involvement of citizens responding to the call for volunteerism, community service and leadership.

All in all, Hanover remains a great place to live and work. But, without question, it's not the town people knew in 1961, one that functioned without traffic lights and direct dial telephones. *(J.D.)*

Before the Grants

For 9,000 years or more, Native Americans populated New England and its coastlines. Sizeable settlements along the Atlantic coast and inland depended on fishing, agriculture and hunting to sustain a vibrant population.

The arrival of Europeans seeking religious freedom and the opportunity to capitalize on the abundant resources of the New World also brought disease. Virulent epidemics wiped out much of the native population in New England during the early years of colonization. As the native population declined, the population of colonists grew steadily.

A series of wars, culminating with the French and Indian War, drove the natives further inland. By the mid-1700s, many, including those in the Upper Valley region, were moving north to Canada or west to New York. It wasn't until 1763, with the conclusion of the French and Indian War, that the region was established as "New England" rather than "New France."

Following the war, Royal Governor Benning Wentworth of the Province of New Hampshire (his offices were in Portsmouth) accelerated the process of granting land to encourage settlement and development of trade and agriculture throughout what is now Vermont and New Hampshire. Colonists from Connecticut, already settled for more than 100 years, had access to the splendid river leading north to the newly opened lands, and recognized the opportunity to participate in the development of land and resources.

The Charter and Settlement

Governor Wentworth chartered 200 towns during the period 1741 to 1767 (70 in New Hampshire and 130 in Vermont). On July 4 1761, he issued the first of a flood of charters from the provincial capital in Portsmouth. (There were 78 charters covering both sides of the Connecticut River during a six-month period.) Hanover, Lebanon, Norwich, Hartford and Enfield were among those granted on July 4 that will commemorate the 250th anniversary of these grants in 2011. Other "Middle Grant" towns chartered during this period included, in New Hampshire: Lyme, Canaan and Plainfield. In Vermont: Hartland, Fairlee, Thetford and Windsor.

The charter for Hanover allocated 22,400 acres, including 500 acres set aside as the Governor's private lot, and responded to a petition presented by Edmund Freeman and Joseph Storrs "in behalf of themselves and as agents for about 240 others…from the colony of Connecticut."

There has always been some question regarding the origin of the designation "Hannover" as it is spelled in the charter. Most authorities feel the derivation is explained by the fact that there was at the time in the town of Norwich,

Benning Wentworth

New Hampshire Historical Society

Eleazar Wheelock

Connecticut, a parish named "Hannover." Others feel the governor may have given the name with direct reference to the reigning line of English kings, the House of Hannover, as the charter was granted a year after the accession of George III to the English throne.

The first settlers, Edmund Freeman and his family, came in May 1765. By 1769, Hanover was home to 157 pioneering settlers.

It was also in 1769 that John Wentworth (Benning's nephew and successor as governor) granted a charter to Eleazar Wheelock, a Congregational minister who had earlier established Moor's Charity School in Lebanon, Connecticut. Wheelock wanted to expand his school into a college but was unable to gain a charter in Connecticut and looked to the north where settlement was growing.

In 1770, Wheelock chose Hanover as the site for the institution that would become Dartmouth College. The new college graduated its first students in 1771. *(T.B.)*

FOUNDING OF DARTMOUTH COLLEGE.

Dartmouth College Library

Dartmouth College President John Sloan Dickey, in top hat, rides with other dignitaries in the Packard touring car driven by Thad Seymour, the College Dean, during the Bicentennial Parade in 1961. Flanking Dickey are Dartmouth professor Francis Lane Child (left), editor of the bicentennial book, and Precinct Commissioner Fletcher Low. In the front seat with Seymour: Precinct Commissioner John Neale. Seymour and the classic car returned for Hanover's 250th celebration in 2011.

Courtesy: Seymour Family

A Downtown Stroll Through History

Editor's note: Frank J. (Jay) Barrett, Jr., has published three pictorial history books about Hanover, his hometown. Jay was eight years old when he watched the bicentennial parade. He has been an observer of countless changes to downtown Hanover over the past half-century. These are some of his recollections.

The Parade

The Bicentennial parade in 1961, a highlight of Hanover's first 200-year celebration, started at the high school, wound up Lebanon Street, turned right onto Main Street, then right again onto East Wheelock Street at the Inn corner, past the shell of what would become Hopkins Center and concluded with a circle around the Green.

Led by Dean of the College Thad Seymour, at the wheel of his classic Packard open touring car, the parade featured floats, marching bands, children's units, and numerous groups, each with a historic theme. Local merchants who joined in the festivities included Harry Tanzi, pushing his father's vendor's cart loaded with bananas and other fruits, and Jack Manchester, driving his service station's antique Model T Ford Gulf Oil delivery truck.

Barrett Collection

Harry Tanzi and the Tanzi Market push cart travel up Main Street during the Bicentennial Parade.

As the bands played and spectators cheered, the bells in Baker Tower chimed Happy Birthday to the assembled crowd. Margaret McCallum, describing the "mammoth parade" in her column in Dave Hewitt's Hanover Gazette, Hanover's weekly newspaper reported, "The parade was the biggest and best ever in this area!" And, paraphrasing the famous Daniel Webster quote, she wrote, "It's a small town, but on its birthday, everybody loved it."

The Bicentennial parade ushered in the next five decades of Hanover's history.

Main Street

The last 50 years have brought about dramatic changes in Hanover's commercial district, affectionately called "Main Street," an area that wraps around to include Lebanon Street. In 1961, local government was still divided into two entities: The Town of Hanover, and the Village Precinct, the compact area abutting the College. Although the Precinct occupied a small portion of the town's 36 square miles, it was the business center of the town.

In 1961, the rural areas were still active farmlands. Town records from 1961 indicate there were 36 horses, 205 dairy cows, 79 sheep, goats and hogs, plus 1,791 fowl. The Fullington brothers, Wilson and Hazlett, had a flourishing business, the Dartmouth Dairy, processing and delivering bottled milk to residents in town. The Precinct owned the Gould Farm, now the site of Trumbull-Nelson, and leased it for $600 a year to a pig farmer. The pigs thrived on a diet of garbage collected from households and institutions alike. Being downwind of the farm on collection day, one was quickly reminded of the resident pigs!

Looking north on Main Street. .

The early 60s brought three sets of traffic lights to the Precinct: One at the Inn corner, another at the intersection of South Main and Lebanon Street, and the third at the intersection of Wheelock and Park Streets. The town's rural character was in transition. The construction of a brick building on School Street for New England Telephone brought direct-dial service to town. Gone was the friendly voice of the switchboard operator who completed each call. This decade also brought Hanover its first primary sewage treatment plant, ending the dumping of raw sewage into the Connecticut River.

Both: Barrett Collection

Today it's the location of the Dartmouth Bookstore. Before it moved to Park Street in 1963, the Hanover Consumer Co-op occupied the space.

Downtown 2011

Hanover, New Hampshire   1761-2011

Dartmouth College Library

For decades, with periodic renovations, the Hanover Inn has been a landmark at the corner of Main Street across from the Green. In 1966, the main section of the Inn, dating from 1889, was razed. The larger Inn, above, opened in 1967. Another renovation began in 2011.

Both: Barrett Collection

CRREL opened on Lyme Road, bringing a major research facility to town.

But, let's reminisce with a walk down (and up) Main Street from the Hanover Inn corner.

The Inn, a keystone at the center of town, had last been remodeled in 1902. In 1966, under the direction of Jim McFate, the Inn manager and John Wayne look-alike, the wrecking ball descended and the modern Inn was rebuilt. In 2011, after 45 years, another major makeover is in progress.

Moving south from the Inn stands the Lange Building, now home to the Gap but long the home to James Campion, Inc., clothiers to many. Campion's shared the building with Granite State Electric, where residents could stop by to pay their electric bill in person. With the arrival of women at Dartmouth in 1972, Campion's expanded to include clothing for women, and a sporting equipment store. Over Campion's was a barber shop and A. B. Gile's insurance and real estate office. The insurance business was handled by Archie Gile's son-in-law, Pete Cavaney.

Bob McLaughry was Hanover's principal realtor.

In the Currier Block, across the alley from Campion's, one business remains: College Supplies. Heading down the street were Art Bennett's Ski Shop, Robert's Flowers, and Coburn's Jewelry Store. Next in line were Lou's Restaurant, and Putnam's Drug Store. Directly over Putnam's was David Pierce's photography studio. In these two business buildings, one could outfit the family in the latest fashions, equip sports fans with boots, skis, soccer balls and other sports needs, send flowers for special occasions, buy a greeting card, and, best of all, sip an ice cream soda at Putnam's soda fountain. It was a one-stop shopping haven.

Just south of Putnam's was Hanover Hardware. Dan and Whit's in Norwich boasts, "If we don't have it, you don't need it," but the hardware store, owned by the Trumbull family, went one step further: Every child in town knew that the basement offered a treasure chest of toys. Beside the hardware store was Tanzi's Market. The Tanzi family offered vegetables and fruits

THE DARTMOUTH CO-OP
JOHN PIANE 1912 FOUNDER

Downtown 2011

1776-1784 — Friction between the state and the towns of western New Hampshire, including Hanover, leads to secession and discussion of an independent state made up of the towns on both sides of the Connecticut River. In 1778 the College District separated from the Town of Hanover and becomes Dresden.

Both: Barrett Collection

The autos define the period--about 1940--on Main Street that was, as now, very busy.

as well as advice, the latest news, and good-natured commentary on the happenings in town. When Tanzi's closed in 1969, the Specialty Shop took its place until the building burned in December 1975. The lot remains vacant to this day.

Adjacent to Tanzi's was the double-bank building, housing Dartmouth National Bank and the Dartmouth Savings Bank. Crossing Lebanon Street was the Post Office, built in 1931 and still holding down that corner today. In 1959, Eastman's Drug Store (it was between Tanzi's and the bank building) moved two blocks south to the 1785 Gates House. In the basement of a brick addition was the Hide-Away Restaurant, a popular hangout for Dartmouth students and teenagers. Agnes Berwick tended the counter and kept a sharp eye on the comings and goings on in town in the eatery known to all as "Greasy's."

Just south of Eastman's was Minichiello's Pizza Restaurant. In the 70s the pizza house was replaced by the Bulls Eye, which became a local watering hole. Several other eateries followed until 2007 when Dartmouth, the new owner, razed these buildings and built the South Block complex that stands today.

The last commercial enterprise on the east side of South Main Street was the Green Lantern Inn, housed in an 1850s farmhouse. In 1959, Al and Kitty Lauziere bought the Inn. The Lauzieres renovated the inn and, though it was affectionately

The Tanzi brothers--from left, Leon, Charles and Harry with Charlie's wife, Harriett--are shown in 1949 outside the grocery store that was a Main Street landmark from 1897 until it closed in 1969.

Downtown 2011

called the "Green Latrine," it was a popular eatery and at times a boarding house where many single teachers, including Bernice Ray, lived over time. The Lauzieres also ran Al's Super Market across the street. They had a catering business and were famous for Kitty's wonderful birthday and wedding cakes.

In 1973, the Lauzieres sold the property to the new Hanover Bank & Trust. In 1985, HBT built the Galleria, home for the bank and other businesses.

Al's Super Market was in an old, wooden building on the site now occupied by CVS Pharmacy. In 1961, A. Wallace Cunningham bought the building, tore it down and built Hanover's first modern food store, the Super Duper Market. To the north was Jack Manchester's service station, now home to the Circle-K convenience store, still the only gas station in the downtown area.

Crossing West South Street, after Dartmouth National and Dartmouth Savings parted company in the early 70s, a visitor would find the new Dartmouth National Bank building and the Hanover Improvement Society's Nugget Theater that opened in 1951. On the south side of the theater was George (Brud) Wrightson's Webster Shop, a pipe tobacco and cigar store, with Ranald Hill Opticians occupying the space on the north side. To the north of the Nugget was a low, flat-roofed structure attached to an aging wood frame building that housed Ruth's Bakery, the Specialty Shop, Amidon Jewelers and Edith Cut Rate Drugs. The Improvement Society razed the building in 1969 and constructed the Nugget Arcade that stands today.

Molly's Restaurant now occupies the next building to the

For many years, Putnam's Drug Store and Hanover Hardware flanked what is now a narrow alley but once accommodated delivery trucks and parking spaces.

north but, in 1961, the occupants were Emil and Elisabeth Rueb's Camera Shop and the Town & Country Shop, a women's clothing store owned by Mr. and Mrs. Frank Lewis. In 1983, Town & Country closed. The space was remodeled by Marc Milowsky who created Molly's as an in-town companion to Jesse's (on Route 120, straddling the Hanover-Lebanon town line) that Milowsky opened in 1976.

Adjacent to Molly's is the Precinct Building, built in 1928 as the home for the fire and police departments and town offices. The three arched windows in the front of today's building were the doors for the fire engines. Cramped for space, the fire department moved to their present location on Lyme Road in 1972. The rear of the building housed the police department and the single office of Marion Guyer, the town clerk. On the

The corner of Main Street and Lebanon Street in the 1950s, before traffic lights were installed (in 1962).

CLEARANCE 8 FT. 0 IN.

PARKING
THRU
TRAFFIC

Downtown 2011

For many years, Jack Manchester's Gulf station was home for both full-service auto repair and a fleet of rental vehicles.

In the mid-70s, Dartmouth National Bank left the building it shared with Dartmouth Savings Bank and moved into its new facility at 63 South Main Street.

Until they were razed in the late 60s to make way for the Nugget Arcade, old frame buildings on South Main Street were home to Ward Amidon's jewelry store, the Camera Shop and the Town and Country Shop.

Clara Sauter ran Edith Cut Rate (named for her daughter) at several Main Street locations for many years.

Downtown 2011

SIX SOUTH ST. HOTEL

Hanover, New Hampshire   1761-2011

Barrett Collection

The Town municipal building was home to the Hanover Fire Department until it moved to Lyme Road in 1972. The Police Department moved to Lyme Road 15 years later.

second floor were located the Town and Precinct offices as well as the Hanover District Court. In 1961, the Precinct Commissioners—Ken LeClair, Bob McLaughry and Lou Bressett—oversaw the daily operations of the downtown area.

The facade and architecture of the Musgrove Building at the south corner of Allen Street has remained unchanged since it was built in 1915 but with many changes of tenants. In the 1970s a barber shop and pool hall were replaced by Peter Christian's Tavern. The adjacent walk-down was Tommy Keane's Indian Shop.

Crossing Allen Street to the north, the Campion family owned the Gitsis Building. After moving their sporting goods business to their clothing store across Main Street, the newly organized Co-op Food Store took over the space. When the Co-op moved to its present location in 1963, the Dartmouth Bookstore, cramped for space, eagerly moved down the street to this space.

The Bridgman Building housed three businesses: Rand's Furniture Store, The Dartmouth Co-op, and Serry's. The Dartmouth Co-op, opened by John Piane as a ski and sporting goods store, was managed by his son-in-law, Dick Fowler. The Co-op grew and soon occupied two store fronts. Serry's, a men's clothier established by Pasquale (Serry) Serafini in 1907, was bought in 1954 by Dom and Sam Zappala and their uncle, Frank, a custom tailor who retired to Italy in the early 60s. In 1985, Dom and Sam moved Serry's to a new building (on a site where they had grown up). After Dom died in 2000, Sam ran the business until he retired in 2004.

The Davison Building completed the block and was occupied by Ward's Department Store. Owned by Bessie Ward and managed by her son, Earl, Ward's offered everything from sewing needs to clothing, housewares, and even bathroom tiles. A young mother could even outfit her children in the latest Buster Brown shoes!

For many years, where Murphy's on the Green is now housed, there was a variety of eateries: the Beefeater, the Indian Bowl, The Wigwam, Scotty's Café and the popular Village Green with its menu of juicy hamburgers and ice cream sodas.

Lebanon Street has undergone perhaps a greater transition than Main Street in the past 50 years. By 1961, South College Street was closed and the site for Hopkins Center had been cleared. Construction of the new facility was underway. East of that site was Roger's Garage, home of a Chevrolet and Renault (and former Packard) dealership, complete with Flying A Service gas pumps. When the expanded Route 120 was completed in 1966, the garage moved to Lebanon, to be known as Hillcrest Motors. Clement Hall was all that remained of the dealership and now that building has been razed to make space for Dartmouth's new visual arts center.

In 1961, on the south side of Lebanon Street, were the Hanover Diner, a paint store (part of Hanover Hardware), and Trumbull-Nelson Construction Company that sprawled over Lebanon Street with its offices, carpentry shop, lumber yard, and the vehicle and equipment repair shop. After Trumbull-Nelson moved, Dartmouth Savings Bank built a drive-up and parking facility. Beside it, John Piane remodeled his family's

Downtown 2011

Both: Barrett Collection

The changing face of Lebanon Street: By 1970, the Town's Public Works Department and Trumbull-Nelson Construction had moved to Route 120. Gone, too, were buildings that disappeared with the construction of Hopkins Center in 1962.

With the expansion of Route 120 during the 1960s, Rogers Garage moved from Lebanon Street and became Hillcrest Motors.

Downtown 2011

In 1985, after decades as a Main Street clothier, Dom and Sam Zappala moved Serry's to a new building on Lebanon Street (on property where they had lived as children). Today the building is home of Hanover Outdoors.

For many years, Allen Street was home to livery stables and then Ray Buskey's Inn Garage.

Looking up Allen Street toward Main Street. Until the mid-1960s, when it was sold to the Town as municipal off-street parking evolved, Allen Street was part of adjacent private property.

1942 ski factory into a multi-use office building that housed Dartmouth Travel and other businesses.

In the early 90s, Jim Rubens bought the Piane Building and replaced it with Hanover Park, an array of stores, eateries and offices. Dartmouth entered the picture in the past decade, adding the twin buildings known as 7 Lebanon Street to house college offices and street-level businesses. It adjoins the town's multi-level parking platform and has created a link to Lebanon Street businesses including the League of New Hampshire Craftsmen, Rosey Jekes, Ben and Jerry's, C&A Pizza, and Hanover Outdoors, now in the building where the Zappala brothers had moved Serry's from Main Street in 1985.

Now, take a brief detour off Main Street to Allen Street and Nugget Alley.

Allen Street was a 19th century back alley until it expanded during the 1960s to create access to off-street parking that now spreads behind the municipal building from Allen Street to West South Street.

Since 1963, 4 Allen Street remains the home of Michael's Audio-Video, opened by Michael Pizzuti in 1942 and run since 1970 by his son, Frank. Along the south side of Allen Street, Roger Burt Printing disappeared in the early 70s. Dartmouth Printing (in the building since renovated and home to the Boghosian family's Gilberte Interiors) had departed in 1965 to its new facility on Lyme Road.

Much change has occurred to the north side of Allen Street. The Dartmouth Bookstore has grown from Main Street westward, first with a two-story addition built in 1974 and, in 1985, into the adjacent building at 5 Allen Street where EBAs is a street-level restaurant. Just beyond is 7 Allen Street, the Buskey Building, that was opened in 1979 by Steve and Ray Buskey, Jr., after their father, Ray Sr., closed the full-service gas station that had also been a car dealership (and before that a livery stable). When Ray Sr. bought the property it included the roadway that he sold to the Town in the mid-1960s.

Nugget Alley, between Casque & Gauntlet (at the corner of

In the late 1970s, Ray Buskey had retired and his sons, Steve and Ray, built 7 Allen Street as an office building that now houses businesses and professional offices.

Nugget Alley gained its name by proximity to the old Nugget Theater that faced West Wheelock Street. The building was torn down in 1970.

Main and West Wheelock) and the Davison Building, gained its name from Hanover's first movie house that faced East Wheelock Street. The Nugget building dated from 1916 and was critically damaged by an explosion and fire in 1944. When the Improvement Society opened the new Nugget on South Main Street in 1951, the old theater lobby was the office for Western Union until the building was torn down in 1970.

The Nugget Alley institution is Walt & Ernie's No Shave, the barber shop in the Davison Building annex since the mid-30s that was started by Walter Chase and Ernie Desroche in 1903. The shop has been owned since the 1980s by Bob Trottier (now retired) who began cutting hair there in 1957.

Dartmouth has been the prime mover in changing the faces of business in town with the addition of the South Block commercial-office-residential buildings on South Street. In 2010, 4 Currier Place (the new name for College Street) is a brick multi-use building just south of Lebanon Street. On the north side of South Street, Church's Children's Clothes and a brick office building have given way for a new hotel, Six South Street that opened in early 2011 and completed the rebuilding of this block.

There are key differences between "Main Street" 50 years ago and today. In the 1960s, almost without exception, residents of Hanover owned the downtown businesses. These owners were neighbors and friends as well as members of Hanover's boards, commissions, committees and associations.

The earlier business district offered a variety of goods and services, from the necessities to luxury goods. Food, clothing, hardware, plumbing supplies, skis, bananas, a skein of yarn or spool of thread, a new Chevrolet or service for a tired Ford were all available within a three-block area of downtown Hanover.

In the early 60s, Hanover might have been termed a "company town" with the majority of residents being employed by the college or the hospital. A college professor, a renowned surgeon, and a carpenter from Trumbull-Nelson, might be found conversing at Tanzi's. And, they would probably all be Hanover residents. By 1961, winds of change were blowing strongly. It will be interesting to see what the winds bring to town by 2061.

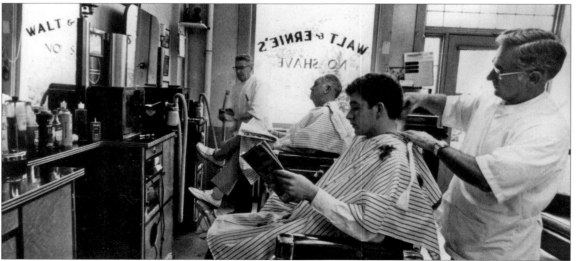

Walt & Ernie's No Shave has been a Nugget Alley institution since the 1930s. Bob Trottier (foreground), who retired in 2005 but still owns the business, began cutting hair at Walt & Ernie's in 1957.

The Town

Jon Gilbert Fox

Brian Walsh, selectman and community leader, relaxes with a brush and pallet.

Preserving Our Inheritance

In 1961, Hanover was an attractive, small New England town. There was no stop light at the Inn corner. The Hop was under construction. Trumbull-Nelson's shops were downtown, behind the Post Office. Falling into the Connecticut River presented a serious health risk. The jail was in Town Hall and President Eisenhower recently had described Dartmouth as "what a college (and town) should look like."

Fifty years later, people swim in the river. There are many traffic lights in town. Trumbull-Nelson and the Public Works facilities are located on the abandoned precinct pig farm. Public sewer and water serve the "village" area of town. Hanover is a vibrant, small New England town with a vital civic life.

Today, we can be proud of our town. Hanover has been the focus of strong economic development forces. Comparable forces have overrun many towns similar to Hanover in the 50s. Our town, with its robust civic processes, and town-gown working relationships, has served us well. We've gained in vitality without loss of the community values that mark a healthy New England town. We can look back and be proud. We have been good stewards of the beautiful town we inherited 50 years ago.

I believe that civic life has been the core of our ability to maintain the best of what we were given while benefiting from the extraordinary economic energy that has been focused on Hanover.

Our journey has not been without conflict and controversy. Many issues have been hotly debated over many years (some over decades). We've been blessed with a tradition of debate and discussion without partisan posturing. In the end we have made good public decisions, in an atmosphere of civility and honest disagreement, with little lingering acrimony or divisiveness.

Without personal agendas and with a commitment to the long-term best interests of the town as a whole, hundreds of citizen volunteers have been the heart of our governing processes. Together they have created the civil culture that is now "expected" in our civic life.

Listing names is always risky. Many are mentioned elsewhere in this book. Still, we should remember and thank them all for their extraordinary leadership and diverse contributions to Hanover over the past five decades.

— *Brian Walsh, Member, Planning Board, 1977-87; Board of Selectmen, 1996 to present*

Town Meeting: Alive and Well

After 250 years is the town meeting form of government still serving the best interests of Hanover? Having served as a selectman and for 30 years as Hanover's Town Moderator my answer is an enthusiastic yes. From our town's beginnings the citizens have elected a board of selectmen charged with managing the affairs of the town from year to year.

From the beginning, however, the citizens have reserved to themselves certain powers. Examples include setting the amount of the budget, approving large capital expenses, approving all borrowing through bonds, controlling the purchase or sale of town land, and since the last century having the final say over Planning Board revisions or additions to the town zoning laws.

Each year the Selectmen are required to post a warning called the warrant. The purpose is to warn the voters that certain actions need to be taken and to describe those actions. The voters gather in public session to exercise their powers and provide advice and consent to the Board of Selectmen. The debate is often spirited and passionate but Hanover continues to be a role model for civility during discussions at each meeting.

Some are concerned at the low percentage of voters who attend town meeting. But, those who attend include a wide variety of voters including College and Medical Center employees, businessmen and women, retirees, town employees—a microcosm of the community. Television, excellent websites and e-mail provide Hanover voters with detailed information. As a result, citizens have a high level of knowledge and general satisfaction and approval of the administration of town affairs by our town manager, the select

Mark Washburn

Harry Bird, M.D.

board and many hard working committees.

The recent actions regarding change in operation and ownership of the Water Company and its land prove that when an issue raises serious questions the voters will turn out in substantial numbers. For those who enjoy trivia, the hours of debate and multiple meetings concerning the Water Company do not hold the record for the longest debate. That honor goes back over 30 years to the meetings and debate over the Town's dog leash law!

Hanover as we know it in 2011 is the proof that our 250 year old system of governance is alive and well.

— *Harry Bird, M.D.*

Jon Gilbert Fox

A meeting of collegial canines on Main Street confirms that Hanover's leash law, passed at a lengthy town meeting more than 30 years ago, is being observed.

Defining Values Remain Fixed

In my years at the College, I have often discussed Dartmouth as a community. It is a community that is physically located in a wonderful place but also one that transcends place, one that evokes a lifetime sense of belonging.

This transcending Dartmouth community also has an address. Hanover is home. Dartmouth has a greater stake in the quality of its physical home, Hanover, than anyone. And Hanover and the Upper Valley have a clear stake in the quality of Dartmouth.

I moved to Hanover and Dartmouth in 1969. The downtown was marked on the ends by the Webster Smoke Shop and the Green Lantern. Over the years I have lived on the Lyme Road, on the Hanover Center Road, on Barrymore Road, on Quail Drive in Etna, and in the President's House on Webster Avenue. My three children went to the Ray and the Richmond schools and Hanover High School. I have felt at home in the ranging precincts of Hanover.

From the beginning I learned that Hanover and our Upper Valley neighbors care about protecting the place where we live and about looking out for those who live here. Over these years there has been a marked growth in the numbers and a wider range in the background of people who have relocated and retired here. And they become part of a community.

My first visit to Hanover was for an interview with the Dartmouth history department. It was in 1968, just a few days after the Northeast Airlines crash into Moose Mountain. I was impressed that each person I spoke with knew someone who had been in the crash and each person cared for everyone who had been part of that horrible accident.

Mark Washburn

Jim Wright, Dartmouth's president emeritus, is a devoted fan of the Boston Red Sox, the Green Bay Packers and Dartmouth athletics, never more than when he congratulated football coach Buddy Teevens after a victory at Memorial Field.

A decade ago we confronted another terrible tragedy, the cruel murder of Dartmouth faculty members Half and Suzanne Zantop at their home in Etna. They were wonderful and generous friends to so many of us. They lived around the corner from the place where Susan and I had lived for 14 years and it is hard to imagine a more peaceful part of the world.

I said at that time that the test of a good community cannot be that it is immune to terrible things. Unfortunately no place has such immunity. No, the true test of a good community is how it responds to bad things. And, in that instance, as in so many others, Hanover—and Dartmouth—stood up, grieved, embraced, and came together, reaching out to support and sustain. In a world of change of which this community is surely a part, some basic defining values remain fixed.

— James Wright, President Emeritus, Dartmouth College

Hanover's Finest

Since the 1920s, Hanover's Police Department shared space with the Fire Department and town offices in Town Hall before moving to its current facility on Lyme Road in 1987.

The room that in 2011 is the Town Manager's office served as the Town's dispatch center. The adjacent office housed three small jail cells. The detectives operated from the basement. The most exciting selectmen's meeting was in 1984 when an inebriated jail inhabitant set fire to his cell. The board meeting stopped and the building vacated. The firemen responded quickly and the meeting resumed after a half-hour delay. Needless to say, the Police Department operated under tight and crowded conditions.

The townspeople recognized the need for a new police facility and soon the second phase of the safety service complex was underway (the Fire Department had already moved).

The past 50 years have seen the tragic deaths of two Hanover police chiefs. On January 30, 1987, Chief Jim Collins was returning from a meeting in Concord and stopped to help direct traffic at an accident scene on I-89 in New London. He was stricken with a heart attack and died on the spot.

Kurt Schimke replaced Chief Collins. Under his guidance, patrolmen were outfitted in new uniforms, the same as are worn today, and a reorganization of the department took place. In January 1994, Schimke was playing basketball when he suffered a fatal heart attack. Nick Giaccone, who was appointed chief later that year, is still the Chief of Police.

While Hanover's police have dealt with the usual traffic accidents, missing dogs, shoplifting and underage drinking, two murder cases have highlighted their work in recent years.

On June 18, 1991, Haile Selassie Girmay, a 32-year old Ethiopian geophysicist, bought an axe at Hanover Hardware, and proceeded to the Summer Street

Ben Thompson, who held various law enforcement positions in Hanover and elsewhere for several decades and was a member of the Board of Selectmen (1977-85), cut a crisp figure when he directed traffic at the Hanover Inn corner for Dartmouth football games and other major events in Hanover.

Both: Town of Hanover

The man behind the beard? Police Chief Nick Giaccone, who has served as St. Nicholas at Hanover's annual Senior Center Christmas party.

apartments. In a jealous rage, he brutally murdered two Dartmouth graduate students, Selamawit Tsehaye (to whom he was engaged) and Trhas Berhe. He was sentenced on two counts of first-degree murder and sentenced to life in prison.

Ten years later, on January 27, 2001, Hanover endured its most highly publicized murder since 1891 when Christie Warden was murdered by Frank Almy, a smitten farmhand who worked for Christie's father.

Two Vermont high school lads, Robert Tulloch and James Parker were cruising Hanover's back roads looking for a burglary target. They came upon the home of Half and Suzanne Zantop on Trescott Road in Etna. The Zantops were much-loved professors at Dartmouth, both known for their interest in young people. When Tulloch and Parker knocked at their door, they were invited in without hesitation.

The boys had purchased two combat knives. While Suzanne was in the kitchen preparing lunch, Tulloch stabbed Half repeatedly in the chest and head. Suzanne heard the commotion. When she came to see what was happening, Parker, following Tulloch's orders, took his knife and stabbed her to death.

The boys claimed they were seeking money to go to Australia but also had contemplated a thrill killing.

State and local police, assisted by Kelly Ayotte of the Attorney General's office (she is now a U.S. senator), traced the Internet purchase of the knives used in the murders to Tulloch and Parker. They subsequently fled the area and were captured in Indiana.

Tulloch was sentenced to life in prison without parole. Parker is serving a term with parole possible in about 25 years.

When this history is updated in 50 years, hopefully no brutal murders will be part of Hanover's legacy. *(W.B.)*

Jon Gilbert Fox

24/7

Over the years Hanover's Fire Department has emerged from a volunteer operation to a professional department manned by highly trained public servants. In the early 60s, the department was housed in Town Hall with three large engine bay doors opening onto South Main Street (the Police Department was located in the rear of the building).

As new and improved equipment was acquired, the need for more room became necessary. At the Town meeting in 1969, it was voted to purchase land on the Lyme Road for a new safety service complex. The present day fire station was built and opened for duty in 1972.

It marked the end of an era: The steam fire whistle atop the heating plant at Dartmouth was retired. The whistle blew in codes, alerting the volunteer firemen and citizens to the location of the fire.

The fire department acts in both emergency and non-emergency situations. Responding to medical emergencies,

rescue missions, and fires are obvious priorities but non-emergency duties are also important including building inspections, fire drills both in town and at Dartmouth, checking hazardous materials and public safety education.

Acting as emergency medical personnel for Hanover and several neighboring towns, Hanover is proud of the fact that all the firefighters are also licensed EMTs, paramedics, or intermediate EMTs.

One of the most difficult rescue missions the department was called to assist was the drowning of a Dartmouth student from Spain, Ignacio Fierro, in 1974. Fierro fell in the Connecticut River on a cold, winter night. After days of searching, his body was finally recovered.

Hanover has been fortunate to escape serious fires in recent years. Noteworthy was the fire in December 1975 that destroyed the Specialty Shop on South Main, formerly Tanzi's Market. The landmark building was on the now-vacant lot between Ledyard National Bank and Citizens Bank.

Irony might best describe the fire in the top floor of the police station, adjacent with the fire department. That blaze was quickly extinguished. *(W.B.)*

Courtesy: Hanover Fire Department

HFD in service, responding to a call on the Dartmouth campus.

Jon Gilbert Fox

Hanover maintains a state-of-the-art fleet of fire-fighting equipment.

Etna's Volunteer Firemen

We built our home on Ruddsboro Road in Etna in 1979. Our oldest son was nine months old the day after we moved in and he walked the day after that. Our house sits on the hill behind the Etna Baptist Church in the field where Harry Trumbull raised sheep and the Stebbins kids played before they moved into town.

Stanley Elder, who came into the postal service almost as a family legacy, was the postmaster at the time. He was also the Etna Fire Captain and Forest Fire Warden, as members of his family had been for decades before him. Stanley was our welcoming committee. He chatted with my wife, Shelley, as she picked up the mail and followed our progress in completing the house and raising a family.

Stanley never missed a chance to ask if I might be interested in joining the Etna Fire Department. The men had officially become a part of the Hanover Fire Department in the consolidation of the Precinct and the Town in the early 60s but they were all fiercely proud of their status as a volunteer department. The Etna Fire Department had won numerous awards at the Grafton County field days. When it came to wildlands fires there were not many peers. After our second son arrived, I felt I had some time available. I took Stanley up on his invitation.

After receiving my physical at the old Mary Hitchcock Hospital, I reported for a drill the next Wednesday evening. I was introduced to Bill Robes, three Elder brothers (Stan, Bill and Jim), Gordy and Frank Hayes (no relation) Nick Pelton and his son, Ken, Tim Bent, Mike Sandoe, Howard Reed, Joe Roberto, Dr. Dick Baughman, and Fred Webster, the Tuck professor.

There were more than 30 men on the roster at the time and three pieces of apparatus. There was Engine 3, a real fire engine with two open seats behind the driver and officer, making for some very cold rides to the old hospital for burnt toast. Engine 5 was originally scheduled to be a Vermont highway truck. It was painted red and equipped with a 350 gallons-a-minute pump and sold with Tanker 1 as a package.

That first night I was the fish out of water. The volunteers spoke a language I was completely unfamiliar with. Sentences were seldom finished. The next person would pick up the thought and a monstrous belly laugh would follow.

Then my training began almost by accident. The fire whistle on the roof blew and something unintelligible to me came over the radio on the grey counter in the station. Dr. Baughman quickly issued me a pair of boots that folded just below the knee, a black fire coat that had John Schumacher's name in it (and a tear through the center of the back), and a black helmet. I thought I must have at least looked like a real fireman. Someone motioned me onto the back running board of Engine 5 and told me to hold on as we went to Blueberry Hill to take care of a small kitchen fire.

Over the past 30 years the department has lost many of those fine men. The group of more than 30 is now less than a dozen. The Etna Station is an integrated part of the Hanover Fire Department. No one rides on the back of a fire truck anymore and members are now paid as Call Firefighters. Now, before you can volunteer, the Town requires 180-plus hours of state firefighter certifications and another couple hundred hours for emergency medical technician credentials. Ah, progress.

— *Lt. John Hochreiter, Etna Station*

The Etna Volunteer Fire Department, shown in the early 1980s, included a cross section of residents who made Etna and Hanover Center their home.

Courtesy: Etna VFD

No Institution an Island

Our family arrived in Hanover in July 1972 when my husband, Dick, started his career at Hitchcock Clinic. We were thrilled to begin our new life in a small, friendly town after city living in Rochester, N.Y., while Dick was in training.

As our children, Rob and Krisy, became engaged in their schooling, I decided to run for the Board of Selectmen (as it was called then). I ran for one of the five seats in 1979 and won by nine votes—not a mandate, for sure. I was the newbie, joining Jim Campion (the chair), Ben Thompson, Martha Solow and Steve Waite with enthusiasm.

Sharon Nordgren

In 1982, Jim and Dotty Campion were driving home from a ski vacation out west when Jim suffered a fatal heart attack. It was a very sad day for Jim's family and all of Hanover. I was serving as vice chair while Jim was away and was elected chair as we all tried to move past this great loss.

Some major decisions were made while I served as the first female chair from 1982-88. Willy Black and Jack Nelson joined the board and we were fortunate to have Cliff Vermilya as our seasoned town manager.

On June 28, 1984, the Valley News published an editorial titled "Hanover Says No" (I still have it on the bulletin board in our kitchen). The Planning Board voted against the Dartmouth-Hitchcock Medical Center's proposal to build a new Hitchcock Clinic on Dewey Field north of the medical school.

The acting chair of the Planning Board, Brian Walsh (stepping up for the chair, Bud Eaton, who was a member of the Hitchcock Clinic staff), in a statement for the Board reported in the editorial, stated, "Neither the medical center nor any other major institution in Hanover is an island unto itself. The planning process of the institutions and the town must be carried out cooperatively to the long-term best interests of all."

To make a long story short, we convened a group of town leaders to continue to discuss the expansion of the medical center and possible options. Representatives from Dartmouth and the town gathered for months. Thinking outside the box, a recommendation was made for an exchange of College property at Sachem Field (where Campion Rink and various recreation fields are now located) and the Gile Tract (owned by the Town of Hanover) that became the site of the new medical center.

Much could be written about this courageous, history-changing decision involving the Town, the College and the Medical Center. I'm grateful I was there to participate.

— Sharon Nordgren, Board of Selectmen, 1982-88; Hanover representative in State Legislature, 1988 to present

Recreation

For many years, youth sports in Hanover were no different from many other small towns-kids (mostly boys) playing pickup games to develop skills. The more skillful went on to high school sports. The most organized activities were skiing, built around the Ford Sayre program, and the arrival of organized youth hockey in the 60s.

In 1973, Hanover's selectmen appointed a commission chaired by Jud Pierson to explore the development of a parks and recreation department. Their report, presented at the Town Meeting in 1974, led to the department's creation with guidance by a committee of seven members appointed by the Selectmen.

The board's first task was to identify a director for the new department. In 2011, Hank Tenney, hired in 1974, remains as the director of Parks and Recreation.

Beginning his career in Hanover, Hank organized activities from an office in Town Hall. With the opening of the senior housing complex in 1976, he moved to office space at 42 Lebanon Street, the newly opened Senior Center across from Hanover High School.

The need for a drop-in center for teenagers was the top priority of the Rec Department. In 1980, the house at 10 School Street became the drop-in center and the department's home for over 20 years.

Program offerings in all areas grew as the department took over the middle school sports programs in 1975. In the 1990s it was apparent that the department needed a larger space. Planning for a new facility began.

Building on the persistence of Tenney and Willy Black, a selectman and charter member of the Rec Board, and benefiting from a gift from the estate of Richard Black, a long-time resident, the Town approved construction of a new community center, housing the staff and resources for the Town's senior programs and the Parks and Recreation Department.

The first problem was finding a location convenient for both students and senior housing residents. Property on South Park Street was identified and acquired. In 2003, the Richard W. Black Recreation and Senior Center opened.

Today, the Black Center is a multi-use building bustling with activity for everyone, from toddlers to seniors, all enjoying a wide variety of programs.

In 1980, the department organized the first Hanover Winter Games, now the Pond Party at Occom Pond. It has also been instrumental in such special events as the Old Fashioned Fourth of July celebration, Muster Day in Hanover Center, and, for over 35 years, the annual basketball tournament that brings over 200 youth teams to Hanover.

The Rec Department has never wavered from its goal to provide diverse and challenging life-long leisure activities for the Hanover community. *(J.D.)*

Hank Tenney has been Hanover's director of Parks and Recreation since the department was created in 1974. Over the years, Hank has also been one of the most successful coaches of girls' teams at several area high schools, including Hanover High.

Recycling

In the late 1970s, Alice Jackson's wisdom and hard work created Hanover's recycling program. As a charter member of the Recycling Committee, Alice spearheaded the program that is saving both the environment and Hanover residents many dollars in trash removal fees.

In 1979 at Town Meeting, voters passed a warrant article to construct a recycling center on the grounds of the Public Works Department. It opened in 1981, a building with three bins—one for aluminum cans, one for glass bottles, and a third bin for newspapers. At the gala opening, everyone was given a free can of Coca-Cola, and invited to be the first to toss their cans in the new bins.

With mixed paper still building up in trash barrels in the 80s, the Recycling Committee collected cardboard, box board and mixed paper at two dumpsters on the site where the municipal parking garage now stands. Committee members were on hand each Saturday morning to oversee the collections. This system worked until it was discovered that high school students were holding parties in the dumpsters, and that

homeless folks were using them as bedrooms.

In 1995, curbside collection was the next recycling venture. Today, residents fill their bins with plastics, glass, cans and all types of mixed paper and cardboard. Pickup is on a bi-weekly schedule and over 90 per cent of Hanover residents participate in the program. Thanks to the vision of Alice Jackson, recycling is alive and well in Hanover. *(W.B.)*

The Water Company

It was a rash of major fires over a century ago that prompted the College and the Town to invest in a public water system. The last 50 years have witnessed remarkable changes in the water system and the purity of the water supply.

In 1962, to ensure an adequate water supply, a third reservoir was added on a tributary of Mink Brook in Hanover Center. Over the years the disinfection systems were modified from continuous chlorination to a chlorine dioxide system, to

the present state-of-the-art filtration system that went on line in 2006. The new facility was named in honor of Dr. William Boyle, long-time water company board member and Hanover's health officer for 30 years.

From its incorporation in 1893 until 2009 the company was owned jointly by the College (the majority stock holder) and the Town of Hanover. With Dartmouth's consent, voters at the May 2009 Town Meeting agreed to acquire the assets of the Hanover Water Works and to operate the water system as a municipal utility. *(W.B.)*

In 2006, Hanover's new filtration system was named in honor of Dr. William Boyle. The ceremony included, from left: former Selectman Jack Nelson; Michael Blayney, Dartmouth's director of environmental health and safety; Dr. Boyle with his grandson, Caleb; former Selectman Jay Pierson, and Peter Kulbacki, Hanover's director of public works.

Adventures of a Health Officer

One evening early in the 1980s, I received a phone call from Sharon Nordgren, then on the Board of Selectmen, asking me if I would like to be Hanover's Health Officer. I was told, "It's no big deal, no work, no job description, qualifications or requirements, but the Town has to name someone." As my dinner was getting cold, I agreed to serve. LESSON: Never agree to anything after 5 p.m.

Then the calls started coming: This day care needed an inspection or that restaurant needed a look. There were very few guidelines as to what to do or where to look. It was an adventure, and I learned a lot. Sometimes I got carried away. To my wife's dismay, I occasionally detoured from an evening walk to check a leaking dumpster or a complaint about litter.

Sometimes I was stumped. I received a call one afternoon that a horse had died in the pasture next to the Ray School. The children were upset. What was I to do? Pronounce the horse? Do grief counseling for the school children? No, just find a knacker to remove the horse.

I was called with all sorts of concerns: Pigeons on the Musgrove Building (they went away mysteriously). Dead crows in various parts of town: Were they a problem? I learned I was in charge of inspecting failed septic systems. No instruction was provided or needed: just a good nose and a pair of boots.

Regularly, I have seen all of our licensed day care centers (great facilities and wonderful caring staffs). Our children are in good hands. Supervision of restaurant inspections was also part of the job. There were lots of stories there. I have had to advise landlords and tenants. I had to evict a pet turtle from the high school and a rabbit from the Ray School. Caring for the health of Hanover was a great adventure that ended when I retired in July 2010.

— *William E. Boyle, M.D.*

Charlotte Ingram

Charlotte Ingram worked in a man's world. On May 1, 1974, she became Hanover's Building Inspector. She enforced the building code with determination and tenacity until 1983, much to the chagrin of many building, plumbing, and electrical contractors. This was a time before plumbing and electrical contractors had to be licensed to do work in single family homes, so it was her enforcement of the code that helped ensure the work met code.

I graduated from Dartmouth in 1974 and began my career in construction, joining Rusty Hyde as a foreman on a new house project, less than two months after Charlotte began her inspection duties in Hanover. When Domus Inc. was founded in 1978, I bought in with all the money I'd saved as a kid working odd jobs.

I learned quickly that Charlotte expected any construction work in Hanover to meet the code. I also learned that behind her demeanor that was sometimes severe there was a very intelligent, warm, caring, inquisitive woman with great strength of conviction.

Her arrival on the job site was with almost a swagger. Some would consider her wardrobe frumpy. She was determined to do her job well and, while she set the bar high, she was willing to help contractors interpret building code. She spent many hours helping me understand the code.

Charlotte had an uncanny balance between an intense, serious, code-focused attention to detail and a sense of humor. She knew she was demanding, and she knew she was not "popular." Her smile, while not always quick, was genuine. A compliment from Charlotte Ingram was much appreciated because it was well earned. I truly admired this woman.

— *Bruce Williamson*

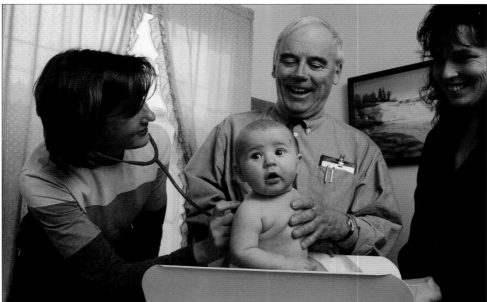

Bill Boyle, a long-time pediatrician at Dartmouth-Hitchcock Medical Center, was Hanover's health officer for nearly 30 years.

Mark Washburn

International Friendship

Brian Walsh, chair of the Board of Selectmen, and Mayor Hisayashi Nemoto of Nihonmatsu at the Friendship Cities ceremony in Japan in 1999.

Towns in Europe have a tradition of having a "sister city."

In the early 90s, Jean Claude Tatinclaux, a Hanover resident originally from Joigny, France, invited students from Joigny to visit Hanover High School. The visit was so successful that soon after a group of HHS students traveled to France to visit the school in Joigny. A group of parents became interested and, in 1994, Hanover and Joigny became official Sister Cities.

Nestled on hills beside the Rhone River, Joigny is a charming French village that combines medieval buildings and old world charm with modern architecture. Its 13th century cathedral overlooks the vineyards that surround the village.

In October 1994, Willy Black, Kate Connolly and Dot King, representing the Board of Selectmen, traveled to Joigny to participate in the official jumelage ceremonies. Soon after, Joigny representatives visited Hanover to repeat the ceremony.

Since then there have been annual exchanges between the schools in the two towns and many other Hanover residents have been welcomed into homes in Joigny.

In 2009, Joigny sponsored a Sister City Band Festival and members of the Upper Valley Community Band augmented by players from the Baker Valley Band traveled to Joigny to represent Hanover. In addition to the Hanover band, the musical weekend included groups from England, Italy, Germany and Joigny.

A Dartmouth president opened the door to a similar opportunity in Japan.

In the 1890s, William Jewett Tucker met a young Japanese man and invited him to attend Dartmouth. Kanichi Asakawa from Nihonmatsu, a town located north of Tokyo in the Fukushima Prefecture, came to Hanover and, in 1899, became the first Japanese student to graduate from Dartmouth. He then earned a doctorate from Yale in 1902. Kanichi joined the Yale faculty but never severed his ties with Dartmouth, and frequently returned to campus to lecture.

A century later, the town fathers of Nihonmatsu wanted to renew their ties with Dartmouth and Hanover and sent a contingent to explore collaboration between the two towns. Proud of Asakawa's accomplishments as an academic, author, historian, librarian, and peace advocate, they sought to honor his life and accomplishments.

In 1998, a group from Hanover and Dartmouth traveled to Japan to begin the negotiations for establishing Friendship Cities. In August 1999, a delegation from Japan visited Hanover and the ceremony was held as Nihonmatsu and Hanover became Friendship Cities.

Each summer, junior high school students from Nihonmatsu visit Hanover and Dartmouth students visit Nihonmatsu to study and visit homes, creating friendships that make the world a bit smaller. *(W.B.)*

Hanover representatives, from left, Dot King, Willy Black and Kate Connolly join officials from Joigny in the ceremonies that joined Hanover with its sister city in France.

Conservation

Hanover is served by two conservation organizations—one public and one built with volunteer support.

The Hanover Conservation Commission was established by a vote at the town meeting in 1966 after the state legislature passed enabling legislation. The Board of Selectmen appoints Commission members.

The responsibilities of the Commission include the promotion and development of the Town's natural resources, the protection of water shed resources, the coordination of activities with private groups organized for similar purposes, and the promotion of conservation education.

To achieve these goals, commission members review lands that may become available for acquisition. They study maps, visit the sites, check market values, and advise the Town on the availability of such lands.

The Hanover Conservation Council is a voluntary corporation. Its membership is open to the public. Under the State of New Hampshire's Articles of Agreement, the objective of the Council is to ensure the preservation of natural areas in and around Hanover, encourage conservation of natural resources, promote education concerning the value of natural areas and how they may best be used and preserved in the public interest, to stimulate scientific studies in such areas, and to encourage land planning for Hanover's future development consonant with the preservation of its natural characteristics.

The Conservation Commission frequently works with the Conservation Council to preserve land that the Council may purchase and hold until the Town is able to appropriate its share of the purchase price. *(W.B.)*

This map shows the Town of Hanover's protected open space lands and trails. .

Hanover has taken great pride in conserving and protecting land throughout the town, including along the Connecticut River.

Town and Gown Memories

The phrase "Town and Gown" was much more meaningful in bygone years. Here are some memories:

• Vermont Transit busses, taking the Dartmouth football team on the road in the 60s, stopping in the middle of Main Street so the Tanzi brothers could deliver a bushel of apples for the team.

• About 11 p.m. on a Saturday night in November 1965 when a large community and college crowd gathered outside Hopkins Center to welcome the Dartmouth football team and celebrate a victory over Princeton that was the culmination of an undefeated season and clinched the Lambert Trophy for Dartmouth, the best team in the East.

• The night at town meeting in Webster Hall when Thayer School Professor Ed Brown, who was also a selectman, gave a 90-minute "lesson" on why Hanover needed to support a bond issue to upgrade our water system. People learned all they wanted to know about turbidity and many had to be woken up when the vote was taken. The bond issue passed easily.

• Frank DelVecchio, the balloon man who, before every Dartmouth home football game for many years until about 1980, ran his souvenir business from the tailgate of his station wagon parked near Hopkins Center. He had a band of youngsters (mine included) hawking his wares all over downtown Hanover.

• The parade of Hanover Public Works and fire equipment through downtown Hanover to honor Jim Campion, chair of the Board of Selectmen and a great civic leader who died suddenly in 1982. The same "passing in review" took place after the death in 2003 of Lou Bressett, another dedicated public servant.

— *John G. (Jack) Skewes, Dartmouth business manager emeritus and former member of the Board of Selectmen*

For several decades until the early 1980s, Frank DelVecchio, the balloon man, came to Hanover from his home near Boston and was a weekend mainstay near the center of campus for every Dartmouth home football game.

Courtesy: Dartmouth Athletic Department

Main Street

"Meet Me at Lou's"

Good food and conversation can be found on Main Street and nearby these days—Murphy's, Molly's, the Canoe Club, the Dirt Cowboy, EBAs come quickly to mind.

But there's only one that has stood the test of time. From the days when Lou Bressett returned from World War II and opened the restaurant that still bears his name (he sold the business in the early 80s), whether they be locals, students or tourists, no directions need accompany the instruction, "Meet me at Lou's."

The restaurant isn't quite a time capsule of Main Street life but it comes close. There have been inevitable refurbishments but the counter and booths are configured about the same as they were 50 years ago.

Gone, however, are the dozens of photos of Hanover businessmen and Dartmouth professors, the regulars, starting with Dartmouth professor Allen Foley (he lived in Norwich), who were honored with a place in Lou's gallery until Lou conceded that, after a quarter-century, times were changing and the absence of women in the gallery was conspicuous. The walls now feature historic photos of Hanover—including a large photo of Lou greeting customers.

For years, Lou's was the place where town met gown. It was where town business could be conducted informally over coffee and breakfast. That still may happen occasionally though the clientele is generally younger, more transient and diverse and the conversation orients toward more mundane topics.

Today, the menu has changed to meet current tastes, a cup of coffee is more expensive, and bakery fare is a feature. But one breakfast item hasn't changed. Under the current owners, Toby and Pattie Fried, two crullers (glazed or cinnamon—warmed, please) remain unsurpassed. In fact, they're bigger and better than ever. *(J.D.)*

Jon Gilbert Fox

Lou's Restaurant has been a Main Street fixture, especially for breakfast, since Lou Bressett returned from service at the end of World War II. The best item that's not on the menu: good conversation.

Jon Gilbert Fox

Campion's

By the time Hanover's 200-year celebration rolled around in 1961, James Campion Inc., known to all simply as Campion's, was already a fixture on Main Street. Established in 1907 by my great-grandfather as Dartmouth Outfitters, the store provided clothing of the day for both college students and faculty. In the early years, sport coats, suits, ties and associated apparel worked well for the all-male student population that was expected to dress in a jacket and tie for dinner every evening. Providing band and glee club uniforms and letter sweaters expanded the store's connection with the college.

As the town and area grew, so did Campion's. With few local retail options available, Campion's added goods and services beyond the needs of the student body. By 1961, Campion's was selling hunting and fishing gear, sporting goods, a variety of footwear, equipment for athletics teams, and canoes for summer camps. The store did dry-cleaning and even sold Esther Williams swimming pools.

More important than the commerce was the metamorphic change of the ever-expanding store as a social crossroads. The staff at Campion's became a family of familiar faces, ready to help with whatever one might need. Customers came to meet friends, pick up the latest gossip, or just to chat and discuss the issues of the day.

My memories of the golden years of Campion's are filled with crazy requests by great customers that were fulfilled by a family of employees that looked after me as a child and educated me as I became an adult and followed my grandfather (James Jr.), father (James III, who died in 1982), mother (Dotty) and uncle (Ron) into the business.

As with all things, change at Campion's was inevitable. The arrival of two interstate highways drew customers to distant malls. In the Upper Valley, discount box stores became a cheaper alternative for buying the union suits and heavy socks I would special order for Knox Tree Service in Windsor (I missed Ralph's take on the universe more than I missed the sock business).

By the 90s, few independent department stores remained. In Hanover the value of retail space became too precious to sell the quantity and variety of products that had made the store a landmark for Upper Valley residents and to class upon class of Dartmouth students.

Sadly, Campion's, the "big store," closed in 1993 when my uncle, Ron, retired. The name on Main Street lived on when my mother opened Campion's Women's Shop in 1993. Dotty kept the valley in classic clothing and quality cosmetics until 2010 when she, too, retired.

We had a good run. For thousands of Upper Valley residents and Dartmouth students, memories of Main Street in Hanover will always include Campion's.

— *James (Jay) Campion IV*

In 2011, the Gap serves customers in the Main Street space that for many years was the home of James Campion, Inc.

1887 — *On January 4, fire on the east side of Main Street destroys the Dartmouth Hotel and the adjacent Tontine block,*
leaving the heart of the village a smoking ruin. During rebuilding, brick replaces wood.

James Campion III, known throughout Hanover and beyond as Jim, was one of the town's most dedicated public servants as a member of the Board of Selectmen from 1974 until his death in 1982. Jim liked to be in the middle of things, as in 1975 when he and Town Manager Jack Stinson (left) negotiated fire hoses in the middle of Main Street during the fire that consumed the Specialty Shop, the aging structure that had been the home of Tanzi's Market until 1969.

Making Things Better

Hanover has been a fine place to live and be an architect. It's fun to think about how things have changed in 50 years. I arrived in 1957 to apprentice with the nationally ranked firm of E. H. and M. K. Hunter (Ted and Peg) and to welcome our first child. The office was in the Musgrove Building overlooking the fire equipment bays at Town Hall so we were at the center of life.

Lou Bressett and Marion Guyer in the Town office ran things. Clinic docs made house calls. The office phone number was 880 and copies were typed. Presentation and construction drawings were pencil on paper. A construction job meeting in New London was a big trip. There were six other architects in town with various interests and enthusiasms. Jay Barrett and Craig Lewis are the remaining family members.

The Hunters moved to North Carolina for bigger opportunities in 1966. Brooke Fleck's office and I joined to design the Ray School in 1968. It was well received and it looked as if we could survive and grow. I had the great luck to find wonderful partners—Treat Arnold, Stu White and, later, Greg Hemberger. As we have retired new partners continue the practice.

Architects try to meet every now and then and the count changes as young architects arrive and depart. Today, there are at least 50 in the Upper Valley doing a variety of projects. All the tools are different but there is a spirit and desire to make things better. That gives me great pleasure.

— Roy Banwell

Main Street Shopping

The storefronts on Main Street have been a moving picture over the last 50 years. So, too, has the merchandise offered by downtown merchants as personal tastes have evolved over the years.

Perhaps the biggest loss for many Hanover residents was the closing of Ward's Department Store. Ward's was the answer to a homemaker's needs. One could purchase a spool of thread, sewing needles and a yard or two of fabric. While buying sewing supplies, a person could outfit the entire family with new shoes and clothing, from underwear to outer ware. When it was time to renovate the home, Ward's had the answer. For a bathroom, Ward's had ceramic tile. Need a new rug? Ward's could offer samples and then install the new carpet. Ward's was Hanover's answer to Dan and Whit's in Norwich—with a much better offering of clothing.

Adjacent to Ward's was the Village Green, a deli-type, drop-in eatery (it's now Murphy's). One could order a hamburger, fries and an ice cream soda to satisfy luncheon needs. This was before the arrival of fast food chains but it didn't matter: The Village Green is remembered with a salivating mouth, especially the free sundae on your birthday.

If someone needed anything for the sporting life, James Campion's had the answer. If Campion's didn't have what you needed, Art Bennett's sporting goods store did. Along Main Street a person could buy ski boots, skis, skates, winter outdoor clothes plus soccer balls, baseball bats and any other sporting need. Every necessity was only a few steps away.

Hanover Hardware, located where Ledyard National Bank now stands, had a wonderful toy store in the basement. All the town's kids could head down the stairs in the Hanover Hardware to gaze in wonder at all the latest gimmicks and toys.

Two drug stores, Eastman's and Putnam's, answered the public's health needs. Putnam's also had an ice cream parlor in the basement, a favorite meeting place for high school students seeking an after-school snack.

Nearly every store in the commercial district was locally owned and operated. A shopper could walk in and be greeted by a neighbor, or a parent of one of your children's friends.

The arrival of women at Dartmouth in the early 70s radically changed the retail base of Main Street, to serve the needs of the new coeds. Change is inevitable, even in Hanover, but the opportunity to buy a spool of thread or enjoy a fizzy ice cream soda are certainly missed. *(W.B.)*

Earl and Doris Ward were one of Hanover's most community-minded couples for decades. Taking over Hanover's only general store in 1900, Earl's father, Carl Ward, built Ward's Department Store into a Main Street landmark. Earl succeeded his father and, until he retired in the 1980s, ran the store that answered the needs of many Hanover homemakers.

1891 — On July 17, Christie Warden, daughter of a Hanover farmer, is murdered in the Vale of Tempe by Frank Almy, a love-smitten farmhand. Almy eludes capture for 31 days, hiding under hay in barns on the Warden Farm on Reservoir Road. He is convicted and hanged in 1893.

Manchester's Gulf

Jack Manchester, my father, graduated from Dartmouth in 1933. He was a Gulf Oil sales rep in Massachusetts until he returned to Hanover in 1942, leasing from Gulf the gas station on South Main Street.

Jack worked seven days a week to build the business. He hired Leighton Swett, a Hanover High graduate, who worked at the station until the late 90s. He later hired Merlin (Diz) Swift from Union Village who had been laid off from the Strafford copper mine after World War II. In the mid-50s Jack hired Larry Hart, another Hanover High graduate from Etna who had just finished military service. When the service station was converted to a convenience store, Larry spent many years at the Co-op Service Center on Lebanon Street.

In the mid-1960s, Manchester's Gulf service station on South Main Street was a picturesque colonial style building with six bays (three in front, three in back). Today, a convenience store occupies the site.

The old station was designed for vehicle storage that took up the entire corner at South Street. In the early 60s it was replaced with a six-bay colonial style building (part of it remains today). The full service station was open seven days a week. In 1957, Jack purchased the license for the Avis rental business that included 40-50 cars and a light truck fleet based at the station.

In 1969, when I returned from Army service as a helicopter pilot in Vietnam, I assumed my father's lease from Gulf. In 1983 my partner (Polaris Properties) and I purchased the site from Gulf Oil and converted it into a convenience store with offices for a tenant, A. G. Edwards.

We subsequently leased the property to Foodstop Inc. (John and Brian Molloy) who operated until 2008 when Irving Oil bought the lease. In turn, Irving Oil subleased management of the property to the current operators: Circle K (Couch Tard, the world's largest convenience chain), Dunkin Donuts and Video Stop.

That's the recent history of one of downtown Hanover's busiest corners.

— *John Manchester*

Jack Manchester, center, and his staff met the auto service and repair needs of customers seven days a week.

Dartmouth Bookstore

If there's a location in Hanover where town and gown truly convene without an agenda, it's the Dartmouth Bookstore that has occupied space on Main Street since around 1875 when it was established by two brothers, Martin and Nelson McClary, recent graduates of Dartmouth.

In 1884, Edward P. Storrs (known as "E.P.") purchased the store from Nelson McClary. E. P. was joined in the business in 1897 by his son, Adna (Dave) Storrs, who had attended Dartmouth for two years. The store was in the new Davison block where the Dirt Cowboy now is located and was known as "The Bookstore on the Corner."

E. P. Storrs, whose great-grandfather, Joseph Storrs, came from Connecticut and did the original surveying to establish roads in Hanover, died in 1916. Dave ran the business until his death in 1953. Wilbur Goodhue, who had been working there since the late 1930s, then became the manager.

Goodhue came to Hanover from Canada in the 1930s but wasn't a U.S. citizen. When World War II broke out, he returned to Canada, joined the RCAF, and flew 29 missions as tail gunner on a Halifax bomber. The war ended for Wil when he was wounded on the 29th mission. He returned to the bookstore and retired in 1976.

Products sold over the years included trade books, textbooks, kerosene, railroad tickets, fire insurance, newspapers and office supplies.

When Hanover's bicentennial book was published in 1961 the Bookstore was still on the corner, now owned by Phoebe Storrs Stebbins, the daughter of Dave Storrs.

It was in 1961 that the Bookstore was brought to court for selling a copy of Henry Miller's controversial novel, Tropic of Cancer. Andy Ferguson, Hanover's police chief, told Goodhue to remove the book from the shelves. Wil refused and was served with a subpoena to appear in the Superior Court in Lebanon. The charge: selling a book that did not have "literary merit" and was "not in accordance with the community standards." Wil was defended by Jack Stebbins (Phoebe's husband) who brought various Dartmouth professors to court to testify that the book did, indeed, have "literary merit." The Bookstore won the case and Wil, a champion for libraries and bibliomaniacs, was found not guilty of selling an obscene book.

In 1963, the Hanover Consumer Co-op occupied space in the Gitsis Block, owned by the Campion family, at the corner of Allen Street. When the Co-op moved to its present location on South Park Street, the Bookstore jumped at the opportunity to assume this large space. The move took place during Dartmouth's commencement weekend.

When Goodhue retired in 1976, Dave Cioffi took over management and the bookstore began to expand along Allen Street. A new building allowed the Bookstore to move westward, connecting to the main store and creating an entire floor for children's books.

In 1985 another expansion occurred, into the Buskey Building at 7 Allen Street, with a separate floor and entrance to the textbook department. A music and video department was born with a final addition, further into the Buskey Building. Now, Bookstore customers can walk in the Main Street entrance and browse through bookshelves spread over about 25,000 square feet, shopping 'til they drop.

Barrett Collection

Wil Goodhue began working for Dave Storrs at the Dartmouth Bookstore in the 1930s. He returned from World War II and managed the bookstore with wit and humor until he retired in 1976.

Ann Stebbins Cioffi sits on the bench outside the Dartmouth Bookstore that honors her grandfather, Adna (Dave) Storrs, president of the Hanover Improvement Society from 1922-49. Ann descends from one of the earliest families to settle Hanover. Her great-grandfather bought the bookstore in 1884. It was owned and operated by family members until Ann and her husband, Dave Cioffi, retired in 2004 and sold the business.

Goodhue had implemented a card file inventory system when he came to the Bookstore, adequate until the size of the store mushroomed. To improve things for employees and customers, the Bookstore became a test site for bookstore computerization. Working with Computac in West Lebanon, 28 computer terminals were located throughout the store, tracking inventory and offering state-of-the-art customer service. Computac perfected the system and reached out to bookstores across the country that eagerly joined the computer revolution.

Over the past 50 years, many famous people have come through the Bookstore's doors. J. D. Salinger was a regular. He often came to Hanover just before closing time to meet family members for dinner. If the store was about to close he would pin a note to the vestibule door telling where he would be. Robert Frost used to stop by to visit a friend, Ruby Daggett, who worked with Dave Storrs as a book buyer. And, Leonard Dilisio, personal secretary to Aleksandr Solzhenitsyn when he lived in Vermont, worked part-time at the Bookstore and shopped for the Russian author.

During one presidential campaign, Al Gore visited and saw a small girl holding a book in the children's loft. He asked if she would like him to read the book to her. Much to the child's delight, he did. Others who have browsed include Isaac Asimov, Melvyn Douglas and Helen Gahagan Douglas, Robert Ryan, Bob Newhart, Bill Moyers, Newt Gingrich, John McCain, Daniel Patrick Moynihan, Robert Reich, Bob Keeshan (Captain Kangaroo), Charles Bronson and his wife, Jill Ireland, Michael J. Fox, Ted Geisel (Dr. Seuss), and Amy Tan.

And, there was a notable window shopper. Early one morning before the store opened, three well-dressed men stopped while one of them scanned the books in the window display. It was former President Richard Nixon, in Hanover to visit his friend, Senator Norris Cotton, who was at the old Mary Hitchcock Hospital. The other two men were probably Secret Service agents.

After Phoebe Storrs Stebbins died in 2002, ownership of the Bookstore passed on to Ann Stebbins Cioffi and Dave Cioffi. In 2004, the Dartmouth Bookstore was known as the oldest independent bookstore in the country continuously operated by the same family. But, after more than 30 years working at the store, the Cioffis decided to retire. The Bookstore's lease and corporate stock was sold to John Schiffman of Hanover with the understanding that Barnes & Noble would operate the store but retain the name, Dartmouth Bookstore. In 2011, Barnes & Noble operates the store and is sole owner of the lease and corporation.

— *Dave Cioffi*

Dave Cioffi succeeded Wil Goodhue as manager in 1976 and guided the Dartmouth Bookstore's expansion for nearly 30 years.

Banking on Main Street

When I returned to Hanover in 1974 to begin a quarter-century as a Dartmouth administrator, I found the local banking scene had changed since my student days at the College in the early 1960s.

The cozy relationship between Dartmouth National Bank and Dartmouth Savings Bank at the corner of Main and Lebanon Streets had cooled due to increasing competition between commercial banks (businesses and checking) and thrift institutions (savings and mortgages). Their divorce was consummated in 1976 when Dartmouth National moved across the street to its new building between the Nugget Theater and Maple Street.

In the early 60s, the building at the corner of Main and Lebanon streets was expanded. Dartmouth Savings Bank and Dartmouth National Bank occupied the building until the 1970s when the national bank moved further down Main Street.

Meanwhile, some local investors had decided to challenge the century-old reign of the two "Dartmouth" banks. In 1973, they opened Hanover Bank & Trust Company in a temporary building at the former site of the Green Lantern Inn at the south end of Main Street.

Otherwise, little had changed. It was still true community banking—local banks, owned and run by local folks, primarily serving the local community.

In the 80s, things began to change in a serious way. The faltering Dartmouth Savings was acquired in 1983 by a Littleton bank. In 1985, First NH Bank acquired National Bank of Lebanon that had opened a Hanover branch on Main Street a couple years before. In 1987, Manchester-based BankEast acquired Hanover Bank & Trust (which had by then moved into their new Galleria building) and then opened a second Hanover office next to Casque and Gauntlet (now the Dirt Cowboy's home).

Meanwhile, Dartmouth National was sold in 1985 to Indian Head Bank based in Nashua. I became a director of Dartmouth National in 1986, succeeding my Dartmouth boss, mentor and friend Paul Paganucci. The Indian Head folks had promised to leave Dartmouth National alone to continue as a locally run community bank.

Any pretense of Dartmouth National being a community bank ended in 1988 when the major regional Fleet Bank acquired Indian Head. Our monthly board meetings ceased to involve interesting and productive discussions about how we could best serve the local community. Instead, we found ourselves listening to a "suit" from Fleet's main office in Providence tell us what to do and how to do it—the Fleet way, of course.

At a Hanover Rotary Club meeting in March 1989, I discussed the situation with Dennis Logue, a fellow board member and Tuck School professor. We agreed that DNB no longer continued its role of being the community's bank. To make matters worse, being directors of the bank wasn't fun anymore. I raised the question of starting a new bank to provide Hanover with the community banking services it had enjoyed for over a century. Dennis agreed it was worth pursuing.

But, we had problems: We knew very little about how to start a bank and, much more important, we had no access to the several million dollars needed to get the new venture off the ground. We agreed on the obvious first step: talk with Paul Paganucci who was then retiring from his corporate job in New York.

The rest, as they say, is history. By September 1989 we had filled out our initial board with mostly local folks including Bill Breed, Lou Bressett, Dick Couch, Leo McKenna, Ann McLaughry and Bayne Stevenson. We hired an experienced and talented local banker, Peter Brown, to be the bank's first president. The board yielded to my urging that the bank be called "Ledyard" to appeal to Dartmouth employees and alumni (John Ledyard being one of the College's earliest and most famous students). And, folks on both sides of the river are connected by the bridge bearing Ledyard's name.

We spent 18 months raising funds from investors, getting the Fed's approval for a new national bank, hiring first-rate local banking folks, and finding a business location in downtown Hanover. After considering several sites, we acquired and restored the Hanover Hardware building.

Ledyard National Bank opened for business on May 22, 1991. Much of its initial business came from customers of Fleet (since acquired by Bank of America) and the other New Hampshire banks that soon closed their Hanover branches. Despite healthy new competition since then from Mascoma Savings, Lake Sunapee and Citizens banks, Ledyard National Bank has grown steadily with the addition of six branches and an investment services division.

Through all this, the bank's primary goal has remained the same as when it was founded two decades ago: to provide the community with "banking the way it should be."

— *Cary Clark*

In 1991, the restored Hanover Hardware building became the home of Ledyard National Bank, Hanover's newest community bank. Inset: In 2008, the bank's investment and trust division took the name Ledyard Financial Advisors and moved into a new home at 2 Maple Street.

Architect's Perspective

The steel frame of the Dartmouth Visual Arts Center is growing on Lebanon Street. This will be the first academic building fronting on a commercial street in Hanover, a fantastic opportunity for the College and community to share in the rich environment art brings to our lives.

Will it be beautiful? We'll wait until it's finished and in operation to come to a meaningful judgment but I wager more than half the community will embrace its contemporary elegance and that will make it a winner in our democracy.

I'm confident it will fit in the community since there are no two buildings alike in the "downtown" commercial area. This diversity of buildings gives the town the solid character that so many visitors and residents find particularly appealing.

The transient nature of commerce has created lively changes within many existing buildings: 80 South Main, originally a commercial mini-mall with the town's only escalator, now houses a bank and insurance company; P&C became CVS; Manchester's six-bay service station became an investment house and convenience store, then a video store and convenience store (the gas has been pumping the entire time); The Nugget has been converted from one large movie house into four individual theaters.

Most storefronts on Main Street and Lebanon Street have had more than one change of occupancy through the years. Ledyard National Bank is housed in a wood building whose walls and foundation date to the 1830s.

Dartmouth College has become a major landowner with property at 7 Lebanon Street; the Dartmouth National-Indian Head-Fleet-Bank of America building; the south side of South Street, and a new structure on Currier. The College has continued the tradition of diverse individual buildings hosting an eclectic mix of tenants while creating a sensitive transition to their residential neighbors in its "South Block" development.

A key element of the downtown and along Lebanon Street will be an open space bordered by Hopkins Center, the Hood Museum and the new Visual Arts Center. This space, void of structures, open to the south and open to the public, has the potential to be the liveliest outside space in town. I look forward to enjoying it in a few years.

— *Randy Mudge*

A work in progress in 2011: The skeleton of Dartmouth College's new visual arts center takes shape, forecasting a new era of activity on Lebanon Street.

Jon Gilbert Fox

Jon Gilbert Fox

The English Lady

I met my future husband, Philip Pierce, when he was in the U.S. Army in England during World War II. We became pen pals. I came to the United States in 1947 and we were married. There was a big gathering outside the church in Enfield, Philip's hometown. I asked, "Who are all these people?" and was told, "They all want to see what an English lady looks like."

We moved to Hanover in 1948. Philip became a carpenter for Trumbull-Nelson. I became a lab secretary at the old hospital until our three children arrived. During the 1960s, I joined Lee Stearns, wife of Russell Stearns, the Dartmouth professor, and Mary Rich, as a greeter of new families for Hanover's Welcome Wagon.

During the bicentennial parade in 1961, I was dressed in Shaker attire and carried a basket of candy. As we turned the corner of Lebanon Street onto Main Street, I tossed a handful of candy to some children. A man standing nearby said, "Look at the arm on that lady!"

I had been trained in sales. With Carol, Philip and Mary in school, I began working at Church's Children's Clothes on South Street (where the new hotel is now located). I also became active in the North Country Community Theater and was in the cast of Fiddler on the Roof with Dotty Campion when she suggested, "Why don't you come to work with us?"

That's what I did for 40 years, first in the women's department at James Campion, Inc., where The Gap is now located. In the early 90s, Campion's closed after nearly a century. In 1993, I moved down Main Street when Campion's Women's Shop opened in the old bank building. That store closed in December 2010. Dotty was ready to retire. And so was I.

— *Edna Pierce*

Main Street Daughter

In 1984, after interviews with Town Manager Cliff Vermilya, Dresden Superintendent Hugh Watson, and Uwe Bagnato, the Hanover High principal, I became Hanover's third Community Counselor, installed on the second floor of the old Senior Center on Lebanon Street.

This was my second job after completing graduate studies but the real preparation was growing up on Hanover's Main Street as the daughter of Emil and Elisabeth Rueb. My parents, German refugees, owned the Camera Shop of Hanover where for many years they served Upper Valley residents and visitors. My father treated customers with respect and courtesy, often foregoing an expensive sale so the customer would leave with photographic equipment that better met his or her needs.

Grateful to his adopted community, my father strived to make Hanover a better place. He would say, "Just because we live in the provinces doesn't mean we have to be provincial." As a member of the Lions Club, he started a "Welcome to Hanover Day" for newcomers to meet old-timers. He served on the Town parking committee because he believed that parking was an essential courtesy. And, he organized Saturday morning concerts in front of the Camera Shop because he valued good music and the arts.

As the town-school social worker, I tried to follow my father's example in treating people with respect and care. Having been born and raised in Hanover, knowing the town and many of its residents also helped. My job involved working with adolescents and parents, with elderly living at Summer Park residences and in the community, and people needing welfare assistance. I had contact with people of all ages.

Especially gratifying during 21 years as community counselor was working with long-time Hanover residents who remembered my parents.

My husband, Oscar Romero, ran the Camera Shop from 1981 until his death in 2006. I stepped in until 2007 when I decided to close the store. Retail and photography, unlike for my father and my husband, were not my passions or strengths. But helping people in need I learned from the example my parents set on Main Street.

— *Dena Romero*

Elisabeth and Emil Rueb came to Hanover as refugees from Germany after World War II. For several decades, as owners of the Camera Shop of Hanover, the Ruebs served the community with a quiet and caring manner, a characteristic carried on by their daughter, Dena Romero.

Courtesy: Dena Romero

In 1990, Jim and Susan Rubens opened Hanover Park, a multi-business facility that helped to expand business development on Lebanon Street.

Downtown Evolution

Since I started doing business in downtown Hanover in 1983, I've seen both extraordinary change and stability. Abundant "shop local" rhetoric notwithstanding, the big boxes and congestion of the Route 12-A strip in West Lebanon have supplanted our downtown as the top-of-mind retail destination for many Upper Valley residents. We took another big retail traffic hit in 1991 with the hospital's move to Lebanon, prompted by the Planning Board's valid concerns over traffic congestion related to hospital expansion.

Our downtown has responded by refocusing on specialty retail, becoming the region's restaurant hot spot, and by dramatically changing downtown zoning in 2002 to permit mixed residential and commercial uses and greater density within the existing downtown boundaries. This zoning amendment passed by a slim 27 votes, with passage sometimes credited to Dave Cioffi and me (we stood outside the polling place all day explaining the benefits of a more urban, flexible, but still compact downtown). Since 1990 as much as half of downtown properties have been rebuilt or significantly upgraded. These changes, along with stable, local property owners who take great pride in our downtown, have made it a jewel among the region's public places.

My experience as a downtown business and property owner has featured an unnatural fixation on parking. My wife, Susan, and I fought a three-year legal battle with the Town (we won a very expensive battle) over grandfathered parking spaces associated with the 1990 development of our Hanover Park building on Lebanon Street. I co-founded two downtown marketing organizations (one in 1983, another in 2005) and later served on the town Parking and Transportation Board, in part to address the 25,000-plus parking tickets given to downtown customers each year.

Perhaps in coming years Hanover will invent a customer-friendly parking system that costs nothing!

— *Jim Rubens*

Parking on Main Street and throughout the business district has been an ongoing challenge for Jim Rubens and many other Hanover business leaders.

The Mayors of Hanover

Hanover's town government has had precinct commissioners, selectmen (and women)—and two honorary mayors, one unofficial and one official.

As the Valley News wrote in 1962, Harry Tanzi served as the "more or less official" Mayor of Hanover, from the 1950s until his death in 1990, With his brothers (Leon and Charlie), Harry was the proprietor of Tanzi Brothers grocery store, a Main Street institution until it closed in 1969.

From the Town's annual welcome event in the 60s to innumerable special occasions, Harry was on hand to meet and greet. He was never better at meeting his obligations than on the October day in 1963 when he presented the ceremonial key to the town to Nelson Rockefeller, governor of New York and a Dartmouth alumnus, when Rockefeller announced plans to run for president in 1964. It was only natural that the event took place on the doorstep of Tanzi's Store.

After Harry's death, the position was vacant until 1991 until the Board of Selectmen voted to name Lewis (Lou) Bressett the Town's official honorary mayor.

As the long-time proprietor of Lou's Restaurant, chairman of the committee that created Hanover's current system of town government in the early 60s, and a longtime leader of the Hanover Improvement Society, Lou was uniquely qualified for the honor after quietly helping to shape the Town for decades.

Lou was Hanover's mayor until his death in 2003. To date, there is no successor. *(J.D.)*

Lou Bressett, second from left, visits with, from left: Hanover businessman A. Wallace Cunningham, Bill Johnson, a Hanover resident who was a justice of the New Hampshire superior and supreme courts, and Walter Peterson, former governor of New Hampshire.

Exercising his duties as honorary mayor, Harry Tanzi chatted with Dorothy Hurlbutt, the retired librarian, at the opening of the Howe Library in 1975.

Courtesy: Howe Library

Hanover Improvement Society

Businesses and Professions

Chamber of Commerce

Both: Flying Squirrel Graphics

Hanover's annual streetfest, organized by the Chamber of Commerce, is a wonderful opportunity for the community to support local merchants while strolling through the downtown business district.

Prior to 1961, promotion of downtown business in Hanover rested with an informal group, the Hanover Association of Businessmen. Their names were familiar to everyone in town. Among them: Ron and Jim Campion, Lou Bressett, Warner Bentley, Bob McLaughry, Brud Wrightson, Pete Cavaney, Emil and Elisabeth Rueb, Dom and Sam Zappala, Earl Ward, Dick Putnam, Roger Eastman.

As the town celebrates its 250th birthday, the Hanover Area Chamber of Commerce remains a relatively young non-profit association of regional businesses. The first U.S. chambers emerged in the 18th century (the Lebanon chamber organized in 1923). Hanover's Chamber evolved as an informal, all volunteer "Main Street" entity during the 1960s and remained so into the 1980s. Since then, organizational structure and delivery of services have evolved and matured.

In 1987, Len Matless was hired as the Chamber's first part-time executive director, serving 160 members. In 1990, he was succeeded by Clint Bean who served until 2006. Under Bean and the current director, Janet Rebman, the Chamber has grown to over 350 members.

During the last three decades, the Chamber has expanded programs and a menu of benefits for its members. With carefully developed partnerships with the College and the Town, and through alliances with state government and regional entities, the Chamber has become a respected organization with wide influence.

The new Chamber has filled a void created by the evolution of the downtown business community. While some local ownership continues, Hanover's downtown retail profile is now dotted with corporate, institutional and non-resident-owned businesses, chain stores, and out-of-town landlords.

In the absence of the resident-owners in the current business community, the Chamber now provides members with knowledge of the area, connections with "key players" and identity and credibility within the broader community.

As the regionalization of the Upper Valley grows, the Chamber—like many organizations that historically concentrated on local issues—continues to redefine itself to serve both "downtown" Hanover and businesses in the region that depend so much on the College and the medical center for their survival.

The Chamber remains a respected forum for business, providing member benefits, promotion and advocacy for community and regional interests. The Hanover Chamber's effort to build and encourage "community" justifies its mission and ensures its sustainability.

— *Clint Bean*

Mecca in the Woods

Traveling east from town on Greensboro Road and onto Great Hollow Road, one quickly comes upon the old Syvertson place, the beautiful farmhouse and several newer buildings that are home to Creare Inc. This could easily be called Hanover's first industrial park.

A "Mecca in the Woods," as its founder, Robert C. Dean, is fond of calling Creare, has brought many leaders to Hanover over the years and has been a quiet (well, not always all that quiet) contributor to Hanover's growth and vitality.

Founded in 1961, Creare has been the incubator for many successful Hanover and Upper Valley companies. This resulted from Bob's unique practice and enjoyment of attracting the brightest engineers in their field, developing them as both business and technical leaders, and then encouraging (some might say forcing) them to leave the nest to pursue their ventures.

Thus, Creare remained focused on its research and development mission while commercialization happened through its spinoffs or by licensing its technology outside the family.

Creare has a worldwide reputation in its main fields: fluid dynamics, heat transfer, cryogenics, biomedical systems, data systems, controls, sensors and advanced manufacturing. It has over 2000 projects to its credit.

Creare got quite a reputation locally in the 60s while working on a jet engine, which it ran from time to time to the dismay of its neighbors. After joining Creare in 1973, I remember getting calls asking when we were going to cease and desist. The engine already was long gone and had not been run in years.

The Creare culture is one of ultimate respect for the individual, a belief that creativity, innovation, initiative and success come from a supportive environment, and that staff at all levels in the organization are professionals in their job functions. Creare is also infamous for its lunchtime volleyball and football games that seem to go on well into the afternoon.

That culture found its way into numerous spinoffs. The best known is Hypertherm, located nearby on Great Hollow Road. When Creare was having its doubts about Hypertherm's potential, Dick Couch stepped forward to develop a world class international company in the field of plasma cutting. Hypertherm now employs more than 1,000 associates in the Upper Valley and has been honored in the state and nationally as a "best place to work."

In addition to being named one of America's Top 25 Most Successful Small Manufacturers by Industry Week, Hypertherm has been honored for its commitment to volunteer service. Dick and his wife, Barbara, are widely recognized for their

In the mid-1960s, this garage at Creare's facilities on Great Hollow Road was Hypertherm's first home.

personal and corporate philanthropic activities. As a company that thinks of its employees as Associates and is partially owned by an employee stock ownership trust, Hypertherm has certainly taken a leaf from the Creare book.

Also nearby is Dimatix Inc (formerly Spectra) that was spun out of Creare by Brian Walsh in 1986. Dimatix currently employs 200 locally as a world leader in ink jet technology now used frequently in printers and copiers.

Another success story is Fluent Inc., founded in 1988 by Bart Patel. Fluent has settled in Centerra and is the world leader in computational fluid dynamic software. The reason so many cars look alike today is that they are designed using Fluent software to minimize fluid drag in order to optimize fuel efficiency.

The Creare family has not only been the source of many well paying jobs, but also of significant local leadership. From Bruce Altobelli and Bill Baschnagel to Peter Runstadler and Brian Walsh, various community boards and civic organizations that address important needs and issues are served by members of firms that grew from Creare.

We're fortunate that Bob Dean found his Mecca here in Hanover.

— *Peter Christie*

Today, more than 1,000 associates have made Hypertherm a world class company in the field of plasma cutting.

On the Outskirts in 1976

It is hard to believe that it's been 35 years since we opened the doors of Jesse's Restaurant. What began is an interim career for my wife Patty and me has turned into a life's work. We were only 25 and 27 years old respectively when we joined forces with three other partners to open a restaurant on the dark outskirts of Hanover on the road to Lebanon. Our only neighbors were Jim's Country Store (now the GoGo Mart), Lester Chevrolet and Wilson Tire. There was no Dartmouth-Hitchcock Medical Center or Centerra Park.

We chose a location on the Hanover-Lebanon town line just to make sure we were fair in dispensing our tax dollars to both the Town of Hanover and the City of Lebanon. To this day, you can be in Jesse's tavern, sitting in Hanover while conversing with your partner who is sitting in Lebanon.

Our only other neighbor was the Lahaye pig farm up the road. We worked hard and long to prepare for our opening in July 1976. With our partners we designed the restaurant, built the building, created a unique steakhouse menu, and staffed the restaurant. It seemed everything was in place and ready for our opening day.

As we awaited the first guest our nerves began to get the best of us: "What if nobody came?" We all rushed outside to check out the parking lot. Down the walk came our first guest ever at Jesse's restaurant. It was one of the pigs from the Lahaye farm that wandered down to see what all the good smells were about. As the first paying guests arrived we were scrambling to corral the pig and return it to its owner. Thankfully, after a phone call, Old Mr. Lahaye came down to collect his pig and we were off to the races. Our first night was a screaming success. We served over 250 dinners.

Admittedly, I've slowed down a bit since then, but the action hasn't stopped (we later opened Molly's in on Main Street in Hanover and Lui Lui in West Lebanon).

But, in honor of our very first guest we immediately put barbequed baby back pork ribs on the menu. It remains a staple and we never had another visit from any of the Mr. Lahaye's pigs.

— *Marc Milowsky*

Molly's, on Main Street, is another of Marc Milowsky's Blue Sky Restaurant Group, joining Jesse's and Lui Lui in West Lebanon.

Still a Great Place to Live

1961 sure seems like a long time ago because the changes and adjustments in Hanover real estate have been quite spectacular on almost all fronts.

When you look at pricing, we all wish we were in Hanover in the old days (if the buying side was your goal). Imagine: 100 acres of open land with breathtaking views of the surrounding local hills and the White Mountains in the distance. A warm and friendly post and beam cape farmhouse with attached el, a lovely old barn, and a couple of outbuildings. It's the North Country dream, visions we still hold today and drool when we see. Priced to sell at $35,000 to $50,000—and that might have to be negotiated down!

Back in the 60s and 70s, Hanover was a sleepy college town. The real estate business trended in the same direction. The few real estate offices in Hanover were small. I joined Linwood and Clint Bean at Webster Associates in 1972 and opened my own office in 1979. Ken Moseley and Blynn Merrill had an office, as did Mildred Clarke, but Bob McLaughry and Bob MacDonnell probably were the town's busiest realtors.

Many were the days when customers would drop into the office and mention a neat looking property they saw in the paper. Could we show it to them—right now? A showing in those days, on a Saturday, consisted of drawing a map, writing out directions with all the turns and landmarks you could possibly come up with, handing them the keys and sending them on their way with a request to please return the key when they were done. It was the easy life for all involved.

Of course life changed in real estate as we moved into the past three decades. In 2009, there were over 170 houses in Hanover valued at more than $1 million. Fifty years ago, only a few of these homes were assessed at more than $20,000.

Demand increased by leaps and bounds. More houses were being built and many of those beautiful 100-acre farms were being subdivided into 20 (or more) single-family lots. Prices began to soar due to the weak supply and strong demand from individuals and families who discovered the lifestyle that was offered in the Upper Valley. As much as we tried, the secret became a loud statement and we, as agents, suddenly had to work every weekend and many evenings. It certainly was an adjustment, quite a change from the "good old days." But, in many ways, it was energizing and loads of fun.

Today, we are in the final stages of "paying the piper" for the huge growth and expanding appreciation in real estate values. For sure, too much too soon can be devastating. Thankfully, the lifestyle we've all enjoyed remains as exciting and inviting as it's always been. It's just the values that need to swing back, not so much to the "good old days" but to a level more in line with how we live and what is offered.

Deciding to make Hanover your home, without question, has to be one of the wisest and most fortunate decisions one has ever made. That part of the equation has never changed.

— Ned Redpath

While many new private homes can be found throughout Hanover, condominium living that began more than 40 years ago, first with Willow Spring and then Brook Hollow off East Wheelock Street and both less than a mile from Main Street, has become one of the town's residential options.

Lawyers and Judges

Fifty years ago, Hanover was considered a good place for lawyers to live but not to practice law.

The legal and judicial scene in Hanover was much different in 1961. There were no law offices in Hanover. The town had its own municipal court that operated from the second floor of the municipal building, sharing space with the selectmen and the precinct commissioners.

The Grafton County Superior Court "rode circuit." The fall term was in Woodsville, the winter term in Lebanon and the spring term in Plymouth. In Lebanon, court sessions were held in the City Hall adjacent to the auditorium that served as Lebanon's only movie theater. When a "western" was the weekday matinee feature, guns shots from the movie could be heard in the courtroom.

The County's Superior Court now operates only from its "new" (circa 1973) courthouse in North Haverhill. The Lebanon District Court has its own building in the Centerra Office Park, covering Hanover, Lebanon and seven other Upper Valley towns.

In 1961, at least four attorneys lived in Hanover but practiced elsewhere. Francis Moulton practiced in Littleton. Charlie Tesreau, Jack Stebbins and Bill Johnson practiced together in the Lebanon firm of Cotton, Tesreau, Stebbins & Johnson.

Tesreau, whose father was the Dartmouth baseball coach for many years before World War II, graduated from Dartmouth in 1938. While at Yale Law School in 1940, Jack Stebbins met his future wife, Phoebe Storrs, a nursing student in New Haven (her ancestors were among Hanover's earliest settlers). They decided to make their home in Hanover.

Jack and Charlie joined Cotton's practice after World War II, just before Cotton was elected to the U.S. House of Representatives in 1946 (he became a U.S. Senator in 1954 and served until 1975). Bill, a Dartmouth and Harvard Law graduate, joined the firm in 1958.

The scene began to change in 1963. Tesreau remained in Lebanon as Stebbins and Johnson opened a branch of the firm in the Nugget Building on Main Street.

Like Bill Johnson, I graduated from Dartmouth and Harvard Law School and joined the firm in 1965. Jack, Bill and I were the only lawyers practicing in Hanover. There wasn't another law office in town until 1971 when Larry Gardner opened his office in the Piane Building at 3 Lebanon Street.

In 1969, Bill became a Superior Court judge and, in 1985, a justice of the New Hampshire Supreme Court. Jack continued to practice until shortly before his death in 1997. He would ride his bike from home to work almost every day and became a leading fund-raiser for the annual Audrey Prouty Bike Ride.

We moved our offices to South Park Street in 1969. Stebbins Bradley PA now has seven attorneys including Jack's son, John, who joined the firm in 1975 and Nick Harvey, who joined us in 1980. Today, we're among more than 30 lawyers practicing in Hanover, not counting those employed by Dartmouth or a bank. Several of us still live in Hanover.

— *David H. (Dave) Bradley*

Not only has Dave Bradley been an attorney in Hanover for more than 40 years, he's also been a member of Hanover Rotary Club since 1970. The Rotary Club, like the Hanover Lions Club, is one of the town's leading service organizations. Dave is one of numerous Rotarians (the club has over 100 members) who take time to raise funds for the club's annual presence on Main Street during the Christmas season that benefits Listen's fuel assistance program.

Printer's Ink

The name has changed but it remains, with the Hanover Inn, one of the longest continuous businesses in Hanover.

Dartmouth Press, the earlier name for Dartmouth Printing Company, opened for business in Hanover in 1843. It evolved from printing businesses dating to 1793 (the Inn and its predecessors date to 1778). It survived its first 100 years by owning and printing a weekly newspaper, the Hanover Gazette, supplemented by printing books, pamphlets, and college catalogs.

In 1899, Frank Musgrove purchased the company and continued printing the Hanover Gazette along with local town reports and summer camp publications. Musgrove expanded the Dartmouth Press by building the Musgrove Building on the corner of Allen Street and Main Street. A footnote: During the late 1920s a future Vice President of the United States, Nelson Rockefeller, worked briefly as a typesetter.

During the depression Mr. Musgrove became ill and the company ran into deep financial problems. In 1938, Kenneth Foley purchased the Dartmouth Press. (His brother, Allen Foley, was the long-time Dartmouth history professor and humorist.) Upon graduating from Dartmouth in 1924, Ken Foley went to work for the Courier Printing Company in Littleton with the express purpose of learning the printing business. He and Arthur Rotch, publisher of the Milford Cabinet, bought the Dartmouth Press and changed the name to Dartmouth Printing Company.

They set about restoring the company. It was still located in part of the Musgrove Building, had 10 employees, some old press equipment, and produced mostly college publications and "job work" for local businesses. As World War II began, Rotch left to concentrate on his Milford operation and Foley became the sole owner.

With the end of the war in 1945 the company expanded into an old auto dealership on Allen Street (now housing

Both: Courtesy Dartmouth Printing Company

Gilberte Interiors). The move allowed Foley to purchase new equipment and establish a steady flow of work by focusing his selling effort on magazines. The first to arrive in Hanover was the Ayrshire Digest of Brandon, Vt., which the company continued to print into the 1990s. This publication was quickly followed by an increasing flow of magazines from New York City. I was hired in 1963 as comptroller and soon began selling, opening up the Boston and Washington markets.

In 1965, Dartmouth Printing left Allen Street when the current facility was built on Lyme Road. Major changes occurred in 1969 when Foley sold the business and retired. I became president and, in 1970, Dave Hewitt joined the company as executive vice president. Together, we purchased the company in 1978. A period of technological changes and rapid growth followed. Dartmouth Printing became a national company focusing on excellent reproduction of both color and micrographs for medical and technical publications.

In 1998 The Sheridan Group of Hanover, Pa., purchased the company. The new owners facilitated the purchase of the most modern equipment available. Today, Dartmouth Printing has 250 employees and continues to compete nationally in the magazine and journal market.

— *Stuart (Mike) Smith*

Press operator Al Stone (left) checks work on Dartmouth Printing's Heidelberg commercial web press that can deliver up to 55,000 multi-color impressions (both sides of the sheet) per hour. Today, 92 pages and 15,000 copies represents an average publication produced at Dartmouth Printing.

Trumbull-Nelson

I've had the great privilege of being associated for most of my adult life with Trumbull-Nelson Construction, a company whose impact on the community over the past 94 years has been enormous.

Founded in 1917 by Walter Trumbull, W.H Trumbull Company, with the help of Dale Nelson, has prospered over the years as one of the major builders and employers in the Upper Valley. Trumbull-Nelson built countless homes and significant buildings throughout this area. Over its long history the company employed literally thousands of skilled craftsmen from the surrounding towns and villages.

Larry Ufford, president of Trumbull-Nelson Construction Company.

T-N was very much a "family" business when I started as a summer laborer while in high school and college. For years the company employed entire families, spanning two or three generations. Many family names including Rich, Stearns, Cook and LeDeau have been synonymous with Trumbull-Nelson. I guess you could say the same about the Ufford family: My father, Len, became an owner of T-N with Clint Fuller and Don Smith in 1966. My brother, Len, worked for T-N for about 10 years and my four sons had summer jobs with T-N (my son, Christian, has been on the staff for the past nine years). I joined the company in 1973 and became president in 1994 when my partner, George Bonvallat, retired.

One test of a successful firm is the amount of repeat business it receives from a loyal customer base. Many businesses in the Upper Valley have survived and prospered because of repeat business. Trumbull-Nelson is no exception.

The company's historically close working relationship with Dartmouth College provides just one example of the value of repeat business.

When I was growing up in Hanover in the 1950s, Dartmouth's Sachem Village was located off Lebanon Street, beside the former elementary school (where Hanover High's soccer and lacrosse field is now located).

Built by the College in 1946 to help relieve the shortage of housing for married servicemen entering Dartmouth after World War II, Sachem Village consisted of 24 duplex structures (48 units). The buildings were expected to fill a temporary need, to be dismantled and sold as housing structures or summer cottages within five years.

In 1958, Trumbull-Nelson was hired to move Sachem Village from Lebanon Street to a new site in West Lebanon. It was a sight to see these duplex buildings divided in half and jacked into the air and lowered onto a custom-built trailer designed by T-N. In the early morning hours, while the rest of Hanover slept, the trailer began its journey up Lebanon Street, then turning south on Main Street, and heading to West Lebanon. One of our workmen involved with the relocation recently told me that, on average, each trip took two days, weather permitting.

Over the years, Trumbull-Nelson has worked on numerous projects at Sachem Village as it expanded from the original 48 units. A few years ago, when the College decided to remove those early units and replace them with new, energy-efficient buildings, Trumbull-Nelson served as the construction manager.

It's fair to say that the original "temporary" buildings served the College well. Many lasted in excess of 50 years!

— Larry Ufford

Trumbull-Nelson was the construction manager for the Corey Ford Rugby Clubhouse that opened in 2005 as the home of the men's and women's rugby teams at Dartmouth. Hanover architect Randy Mudge designed the distinctive building named for Corey Ford, the noted writer who came to Hanover in 1952, a year after the rugby club was organized. Ford said, "Rugby took me up," and, until his death in 1969, his home on North Balch Street was the club's adopted headquarters.

Barrett Collection

This aerial view dramatically illustrates how the area of Hanover along Lebanon Street has changed since the 1950s. In 1958, Trumbull-Nelson relocated Sachem Village, beside Hanover High and Hanover Elementary schools, to its current site in West Lebanon. Sachem Village was the housing development built by Dartmouth College to house married veterans returning from World War II. Today, the elementary school is part of Hanover High which looks much different. The only easily recognized landmarks are St. Denis Church and a corner of Dartmouth's Memorial Field.

AMCA International

When Kenneth Barclay and two associates arrived in Hanover from Montreal in the early 70s and rented modest second-floor office space on Allen Street, only the landlord noticed.

In 1989, when Bill Holland, Barclay's successor as chief executive of the company called AMCA International (it became United Dominion Industries in 1990), announced plans to relocate the corporate headquarters group to Charlotte, N.C., the news sent ripples through Hanover and the Upper Valley.

There was always an air of mystery about AMCA (an acronym for AMerica-CAnada). Barclay (who retired in 1986) and then Holland guided a group that used Hanover as a base of operations to expand a company that grew out of Dominion Bridge, for more than a century Canada's leading steel fabricator and construction company that was struggling to survive.

The group operated from offices in Hanover and Lebanon for the U.S. subsidiary of Dominion Bridge to execute a growth by acquisition strategy that reached across North America and beyond.

When Barclay arrived in 1973, Dominion Bridge had annual sales of $278 million. When Holland and about 35 AMCA families (in a flurry of real estate transactions) moved to Charlotte, sales were $1.4 billion for a company with 10,000 employees and 34 operating locations. When United Dominion was acquired by SPX Corporation in 2001, sales had grown to $2.3 billion.

Gone, too, with AMCA's departure, was a deep-pockets company that quietly donated thousands of dollars annually to benefit education, recreation, the arts and medicine in the Upper Valley. Most visible and enduring among AMCA's philanthropic interests (corporate and personal) are the same-day surgical unit at Dartmouth-Hitchcock Medical Center in Lebanon and the pre-engineered building that is now Campion Rink.

For many years, the Hanover Chamber of Commerce has recognized a Citizen of the Year. It was always awarded to an individual until 1989 when, as AMCA prepared to depart, the company was cited for the honor. *(J.D.)*

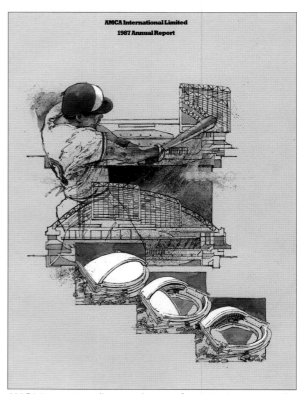

AMCA International's annual report for 1987 shows one of the company's notable projects at that time: steel fabrication for the retractable-roof Skydome (now the Rogers Centre) that became the home of the Toronto Blue Jays. AMCA moved its headquarters from Hanover to Charlotte, N.C., in 1989.

One of AMCA International's significant donations to the Upper Valley was the pre-engineered building that is now the James Campion III Rink. A community project led by the Hanover Improvement Society, the rink replaced Dartmouth's Davis Rink as a home for youth hockey and other skaters. The ice-making equipment, donated by the College, came from Davis Rink and continues in operation.

Dotty Campion, widow of Jim Campion who died in 1982, skates with her granddaughter, Ashley (daughter of Jay Campion), during the dedication event for the James Campion III Rink in February 1988.

CRREL

In 1961, ground was broken to construct an engineering facility in Hanover. The new complex, the U.S. Army's Cold Regions Research and Engineering Laboratory, known to all as CRREL, combined two government laboratories: the Arctic Construction and Frost Effects Laboratory and SIPRE (Snow, Ice, and Permafrost Research Establishment). Organizers of this facility included the U.S. Army, Dartmouth President John Sloan Dickey, and New Hampshire's two senators, Norris Cotton and Styles Bridges. Dartmouth encouraged the plan by offering land on Lyme Road for one dollar a year for 100 years.

A massive fire delayed opening of the facility until November 1963. The new facility and its talented engineers soon became pioneers in ice study. They were the first to penetrate the Greenland ice shield and several years later, the Antarctic ice shield.

Over nearly five decades, CRREL engineers have traveled around the world as leaders in research and scientific discovery involving cold weather and ice patterns. (W.B.)

Jon Gilbert Fox

CRREL has expanded dramatically along the west side of Lyme Road since the Army's facility opened in Hanover in 1963. This aerial view also shows development in that area: At the upper left is Dartmouth Printing Company. At the upper right is the Richmond Middle School.

The College

Adrian Bouchard

Hanover's holiday season was never more colorful than during the 1960s when the Christmas trees bordered the Dartmouth Green. This view, from the tower of Baker Library looking toward Hopkins Center and the Hanover Inn, was taken by Adrian Bouchard, the College photographer from 1937 to 1976.

The Wheelock Succession

Beginning with Eleazar Wheelock, who founded Dartmouth College in 1769, there have been 17 presidents of the College in the Wheelock Succession including six during the past 50 years.

John Sloan Dickey (left) was Dartmouth's president from 1945-70, leading the College through post-World War II growth. He retired soon after the College celebrated its bicentennial in 1969. John G. Kemeny (right), a mathematics professor until he became president (he was also a member of the Hanover and Dresden school boards in the 1960s), served from 1970-81. His tenure was marked by the arrival of women as undergraduates at the College and the beginning of a year-round academic calendar, both in 1972.

James O. Freedman (left), president from 1987-98, guided a plan that elevated Dartmouth's academic standing in the Ivy League and beyond. Freedman is shown with President Bill Clinton, the commencement speaker in 1995 whose presence drew more than 15,000 people to Hanover and prompted the ceremony to be moved from the Green to Memorial Field.

James Wright and his wife, Susan, leave the stage after Wright's last commencement in 2009. Wright served 11 years as president, concluding over 40 years at Dartmouth that began when he arrived as an assistant professor of history. Wright presided over a period of significant new construction throughout the campus. He said, "I may be the only one on campus who still thinks of myself as a historian and faculty member, but that's who I am."

David T. McLaughlin (right), president from 1981-87, was instrumental in plans that led to the relocation of Dartmouth-Hitchcock Medical Center. McLaughlin is shown presenting an honorary master's degree to Hanover business leader Lou Bressett (left) during Dartmouth's commencement in 1986. Between Bressett and McLaughlin is long-time mathematics professor Bill Slesnick.

Since becoming president in 2009, Jim Yong Kim has already made his mark at Dartmouth with the introduction of several academic initiatives while also presiding over a period of adjustment to restore the College's fiscal standing in the aftermath of national economic downturn that began in 2008.

"The Hop"

Named for Ernest Martin Hopkins, Dartmouth's president from 1916-45, Hopkins Center has been a focal point of the arts at the College and in the Upper Valley since it opened in 1962.

The opening of the Hopkins Center for the Creative and Performing Arts on November 8, 1962 produced a sea change in the Hanover and Upper Valley cultural landscape. As its 50th anniversary approaches "The Hop" remains one of the most vibrant buildings on the Dartmouth campus—and a popular destination for art lovers throughout the region.

Built to provide a modern and technically unsurpassed home for Dartmouth's scattered drama, music and art venues, the Hop fostered many unanticipated major impacts on the life of the community under the watchful eye of its first director, Warner Bentley.

Designed to expose Dartmouth students to the wonders of the arts during their daily visits to the strategically located post office, the Hop offered similar exposure to the Hanover community. Anyone walking through the Hop to avoid bad weather or to attend a performance passed several art galleries, or studios and auditoria where coming artistic attractions were advertised.

Dartmouth students en route to exams have rubbed (for good luck) the nose of the bronze bust that honors Warner Bentley, the first director of Hopkins Center.

Stuart Bratesman

When he's not on occasional display in Hopkins Center, Rudolph the red-nosed reindeer resides in the College archives. The story of Santa's ninth reindeer was the creation of Robert L. May, Dartmouth Class of 1926, who wrote the tale of Rudolph for a seasonal booklet published by Montgomery Ward, the retailer, in 1939.

Joseph Mehling

From the early 1980s until 2009 when it decided to perform only in areas with dense population, the Big Apple Circus was an annual summer spectacle in Hanover sponsored by the Hopkins Center. The European-style one-ring circus, set up in recent years at the old Fullington Farm field on Lyme Road, was co-founded in 1977 by Paul Binder, Dartmouth Class of 1963.

Then, as now, one passing through could hear singing and instrumental groups rehearsing or observe the theater crew building sets for an upcoming dramatic presentation. Dinners and social gatherings scheduled in the Top of the Hop or Alumni Hall brought many in touch with the cultural offerings of the College.

The Hop provided local performers like Dotty Campion, Edna Pierce and Peggy Cooperman—to name a few—an opportunity to perform on a stage that rivaled the best in New York.

Hanover residents were welcome to join in classes in the Center's woodworking and metalworking shops, and its lapidary. For a fee they could enroll in drawing and painting courses, under the direction of a visiting artist, in the Hop's studios.

In its initial years, the summer Congregation of the Arts presented a smorgasbord of plays, concerts and art exhibits developed around a central theme. A talented repertory company and the Dartmouth Symphony Orchestra, enhanced by students from New York's Julliard School, provided entertainment of professional quality.

The Hop introduced arts, drama and culture to students in Hanover's public schools and throughout the Upper Valley. Hanover offered not only the characteristics of a typical New England college town but added cultural and educational advantages matched by few communities.

Over the years, Hanover has moved to the top of virtually every list that recommended "the best places to retire." Dartmouth alumni and those from many other prestigious colleges and universities chose to move to Hanover and join one of the growing number of retirement communities—

Kendal, Wheelock Terrace, Hanover Greens, and others located throughout the Upper Valley.

The community has benefited from all of these opportunities—and responded in kind. Hundreds of volunteers from the community support the Hopkins Center and the Hood Museum (which opened in 1985) in their artistic endeavors and contribute generously to their programs.

The interest in the arts generated by the Hop's programs helped encourage the emergence of performing groups and organizations throughout the Upper Valley, adding to the quality of life that is so precious to Hanover and its neighbors.

The Hop has achieved, and surpassed, the vision of Warner Bentley and his colleagues that led to its creation in 1962. (T.B.)

Hanover Improvement Society

Tom Byrne, Dartmouth Class of 1955, was the Hopkins Center business manager when it opened in 1962. From 1966-91, he was associate director of Computing Services at Dartmouth and, from 1991-2007, Tom was general manager of the Hanover Improvement Society. A community leader and a member of the committee that produced this book, Tom has played a major role in organizing Hanover's 250th birthday celebration.

Digital Pioneers

As young professors of mathematics at Dartmouth in the 1960s, Tom Kurtz (left) and John Kemeny were driving forces in the development of computing at Dartmouth and beyond.

Dartmouth College's presence in Hanover, especially near its schools, provided the Town with a head start on the computer revolution and the concepts of personal computing and networking.

The first known remote use of a computer occurred on the Dartmouth campus in 1940 and the concept of artificial intelligence was first articulated at Dartmouth in 1956.

By the 1960s, led by Dartmouth professors John Kemeny (later the College's 13th president) and Tom Kurtz, development of the simple BASIC language, and the easy-to-use Dartmouth Time-Sharing System (DTSS) attracted national attention and federal support for several National Science

Foundation projects. Among these was one that linked seven secondary schools in New England to DTSS to explore the integration of computing and programming into the curriculum.

Hanover High School was among the participants with math teachers Mary Hutchins and Bill Cogswell coordinating the effort. Hanover was joined in this effort by Mascoma and Lebanon high schools along with Phillips Andover, Phillips Exeter, Northfield-Mount Hermon and Vermont Academy.

Although the terminals and network configurations were primitive, the concepts and applications were similar to today's technology. There were computer games, the early equivalent of chat rooms, e-mail programs, and a rapidly developing library of accessible applications, databases, and even texts. All, of course, were accessed at agonizingly slow speeds.

The number of terminals on the network grew quickly as speed and capacity of the central computers improved. At its height, DTSS could handle over 200 users at one time. This experiment was a precursor to the Dartmouth Educational Network, which, at its peak, served 30 colleges and 20 secondary schools in New England, 12 colleges in Canada (over dedicated teletype terminals), and scores of educational and research organizations over national commercial networks.

In Hanover, the system encouraged the development of applications that eventually spurred advancements in the diagnosis and treatment of cancer patients and contributed to the founding of the Norris Cotton Cancer Center. Tuck School professors developed applications to manage investments and local government used the system to select juries. An application was written to compute an individual's federal income tax for 1970. The results of elections were predicted using a BASIC program and information for exit interviews at key polling places. Monthly payments and interest on a mortgage loan were computed using BASIC programs written by Dartmouth students and faculty.

The endless possibilities for applying the new technology to every facet of life were unveiled. With this widespread symbiosis of computer technology and human ingenuity "a thousand flowers bloomed."

Professors and administrators soon had teletype terminals in their homes and their families enjoyed access to DTSS in the 70s and 80s. Entrepreneurial Dartmouth graduates with strong computing skills often stayed in the region to maintain access to computing. They formed companies specializing in banking, investments and other businesses that were obvious candidates for computerization and personal computing.

Some computer literate high school graduates who invested many hours writing programs went on to Dartmouth or with local businesses, developing sophisticated software applications.

Thanks to Dartmouth's pioneering efforts, Hanover was one of the earliest "wired" Towns in the nation.

By the early 80s, the networks were faster and connected to the nationwide, but fledgling, Internet. They often contained logic of their own that made them even more utilitarian. The

Adrian Bouchard

personal computer, made possible by the invention of the microchip, became a reasonable option for those seeking to escape the limitations of slow-speed phone lines and the limited capacity and speed of their terminals. (All of the first personal computers had to be programmed by their users and hobbyists in the BASIC language that functioned efficiently in the limited memory of the early microcomputers.)

Personal computers appeared in significant numbers in the early 80s. In 1984, Apple introduced its Macintosh computer and Dartmouth became one of the first colleges to require that every first-year student purchase a Macintosh. In Hanover, Macs rapidly spread to homes, laboratories, businesses and school classrooms that were later joined by a wide range of ever-less-expensive personal computers.

Dartmouth capitalized on the microcomputer's stand-alone capability by developing software in the DTSS operating system that allowed personal computers to also serve as smart terminals, accessing the larger and much more powerful DTSS central computer. The campus networks, and those throughout Hanover, were constantly upgraded to handle higher transmission rates and new graphical applications.

From 1966 until the late 90s when it had become a victim of time and was demolished to make way for the Berry Library, Kiewit Computation Center housed the massive computer that was the hub of academic computing at Dartmouth. The building, a gift of Peter Kiewit, Dartmouth Class of 1922, was built by Trumbull-Nelson for $650,000. The first GE-635 computer in Kiewit cost $2.5 million.

Hanover embraced personal computing and networking in the 60s, fostering a technically savvy population that has served the Town well over the past 50 years. Today, there is no accounting for the number of computers in Hanover—in schools, homes, offices, theatres, libraries, autos and cell phones. Folks strolling along the streets of Hanover have more computer power at their fingertips than the pioneers in 1964 had in the DTSS central computer.

Thanks to John Kemeny, Tom Kurtz, generations of imaginative Dartmouth student programmers, and creative high school students, Hanover's citizens were more than ready to adapt to the digital world in the 21st century and its global electronic social networks. (T.B.)

During his tenure as president of Dartmouth in the 1970s, John Kemeny stood with a computer disk between the rows of card files that were the source to find books in Baker Library. Kemeny's message: That before long the information in the card files would be condensed and available on a disk.

Times Have Changed

It's always difficult to compare today with any time in the past. Folks don't realize that, in reality, life goes on more or less the same. It's only the details and magnitudes that change.

Taking a crack at the magnitude of change in information technology should be couched in terms familiar to younger folks today. So, consider the novel as a measurement tool. How many novels can be stored on whatever and how long does it take to download a novel?

Let's ignore internal memory, access time and processor speeds. Folks don't use computers to add numbers anymore. They use computers to watch movies.

So, how does one compare what we had in 1966 (actually, around 1970 when the system was finally completed)?

First, compare storage memory (letters, books, movies, songs, etc.). Memory is usually measure in bytes. One byte is enough memory to contain a letter, digit, or punctuation mark. A typical short novel might contain 200 pages. Each page contains about 300 words. An average word contains six letters (counting the spaces between words). Since one letter requires one byte of memory, that comes to about 360,000 bytes. So, let's use this "novel" as our basic measure of computer memory.

The 1970 version of DTSS included 340 million words of storage memory. A "word" in those days amounted to about four bytes, for a total of 1.36 billion bytes. Thus, you could store about 4000 short novels.

A recent advertisement for a Computer Tablet boasted 32 gigabytes of storage. That comes to about 90,000 novels, a storage improvement of more than 20-to-1. But, it must be remembered that the 1970 DTSS served the entire Dartmouth community plus numerous nearby colleges and secondary schools.

The 1970 version of DTSS cost about $2.5 million, not counting its huge building or the staff required to keep it running. In 2011, the typical Tablet costs about $600. Thus, the cost to store a novel in 1970 would have been at least $600 while the same cost in 2011 would be less than one cent. That's a pretty big improvement.

What about download speed?

A Teletype terminal in those days was capable of handling 10 bytes per second. If one user were interested in downloading a novel at that rate, it would have taken about 10 hours. At today's download speeds, which might typically be something like 2 GHz, the same downloading would take about 1.5 seconds.

Also, remember that in 1970 a user needed access to a Teletype terminal connected to DTSS by a telephone line. In 2011, the same user can be anywhere, including on a bus ride to New York City or a bench on Main Street, and be connected at all times with no wires.

Around Hanover or wherever, times have changed.

— *Tom Kurtz*

In 2011, Tom Kurtz sits on a Main Street bench with a Tablet computer, a measure of the changes he has seen since he helped to launch the computer revolution at Dartmouth in the 1960s.

Jon Gilbert Fox

Spike Chamberlin and the Parkhurst Takeover

It was mid-afternoon on May 6, 1969. I was the associate business manager at Dartmouth and in my office in Parkhurst Hall when Students for a Democratic Society, a radical group during the Vietnam War years, stormed the building. The SDS demanded that the building be vacated immediately.

There was a lot of confusion before Dean Thad Seymour passed the word to all offices that we should vacate. After a lot of foot dragging we all left except for Waldo (Spike) Chamberlin, dean of Summer Programs. I think Spike was the oldest College officer in the building and he wasn't about to be told what to do by a ragtag bunch of students.

By about 4 p.m., there was a big crowd outside Parkhurst—students, staff, community onlookers, campus and Hanover police, and the press. For two hours people with authority tried to talk Spike into leaving. His office was in the basement on the northeast corner of the building and there was Thad Seymour, on his hands and knees, talking to Spike through a window and trying to convince him to leave.

Spike said he still had work to do and wasn't leaving until his day's work was done. About 6:30 p.m., he packed his briefcase, turned off the lights and left. In retrospect, he was a hero for many of us.

— *John G. (Jack) Skewes, Business Manager Emeritus, Dartmouth College*

By late afternoon on May 6, 1969, student protesters intent on abolishing ROTC and military recruiting at Dartmouth were sitting on the windowsills in the office of President John Sloan Dickey after taking over Parkhurst Hall. The protest continued until the students were removed by state and local police. While the protest developed, an intramural softball game continued uneventfully across the street on the Green.

ILEAD

The spark for ILEAD, the Institute for Lifelong Education at Dartmouth, ignited in 1989 with a proposal from Steve Calvert of the College's alumni relations staff to John Strohbehn, then Dartmouth's provost.

Calvert's office was being overwhelmed by requests from Hanover's growing population of retirees, including many Dartmouth alumni, to audit undergraduate courses. In November 1990, with the encouragement of Mike McGean, former secretary of the College, and influenced by John Lincoln, a long-time Hanover High history teacher, Calvert and 38 members of the Hanover community established ILEAD.

ILEAD was modeled after a movement at the New School of Research in New York City along with a program at Harvard and the five-college "Learning in Retirement" program in western Massachusetts.

The Institute is designed to present thought-provoking discussion programs that are self-administered and peer taught. Since 1990, there have been over 1,500 study groups with an enrollment of over 25,000 students.

ILEAD is a self-supporting department at Dartmouth with offices housed in the Dartmouth Outing Club House. ILEAD's format now is similar to programs at 300 other colleges and universities and, with over 1,400 current members, is the sixth largest program in the United States.

Between 35 and 50 study groups are offered during the fall, winter and spring terms. Classes run from five to eight weeks with subjects ranging from politics and history to art, literature, theater, science, ethics, music, writing and spirituality.

ILEAD's summer lecture series offers lectures for six to eight weeks on subjects of current interest. In addition to the regular study sessions, ILEAD offers study-travel programs to visit countries worldwide and also offers a series of day and overnight trips to historical sites and cultural events. *(W.B.)*

In April 1991, Steve Calvert (left) joined James Freedman, Dartmouth's president (center), and Tom Campion, a founder and first president of ILEAD, to sign the charter for ILEAD that in 2011 continues as one of the Hanover area's leading resources for continuing education.

Mutual Trust and Respect

Over many years the College and the Town have had a strong sense of mutual trust and respect fostered by constant communication that seldom breaks down. I'm told this was not always so.

In my almost 40 years in facilities planning at Dartmouth, prior to retiring in 2001, it was my responsibility, with others, to be sure Dartmouth maintained and strengthened that trust and respect. Informal communication, almost daily and more frequently when necessary, between our group and the Town staff and boards ensured against surprises. It usually worked, but not always.

One day in the early 1980s a College maintenance person who worked at the Medical School told me that the DMS administration had planned, contracted for, and begun substantial interior renovations to one of its buildings in Hanover. I had no knowledge of the project.

In those days the med school did much of its own planning and contracting. This project had no Town permits. There had been no contact with the Town. This was neither right nor legal nor in keeping with our goal of mutual trust.

I did two things that morning. I told the DMS administration to stop the project. Then I called Cliff Vermilya, the town manager. We met that day and set a direction to secure the necessary permits and delay the work as little as possible. Within a week Cliff arranged for the appropriate Town departments to review the project after my office and the DMS administration had completed the permit applications.

We worked together to solve the problem and the project was completed with little delay. This may not be a unique relationship between an institution and the town it is in but it is rare that it is as solid as we have had it in Hanover.

— Gordon DeWitt, Director of Facilities Planning Emeritus, Dartmouth College

Golden Years

Sports, whether at Dartmouth or Hanover High, have been an important part of life in Hanover for years. But there was something very special about the years from 1961 to 1970 when Coach Bob Blackman's Dartmouth teams dominated Ivy League football. His teams were the talk of the town—and far beyond.

Blackman was a coaching genius, on the field and off. He took over a struggling program in 1955 and immediately instituted a national recruiting program that was foreign to the Ivy League. From 1955-70, when he left for Illinois and the Big Ten, his teams won seven Ivy League championships, had three undefeated seasons, and twice won the Lambert Trophy as the East's best team.

These were the years when a Friday night bonfire on the Green preceded every home game. There were rallies that brought townspeople and students together to send the team on the road and again to celebrate victories when the busses returned across the Ledyard Bridge.

More often than not, Dartmouth was a regular on CBS, NBC and ABC regional telecasts (before the days of ESPN and countless games on cable) for games at Harvard, Yale and Princeton, traditionally road games for Dartmouth until Memorial Field was expanded to over 20,000 seats in 1968, setting up a home-and-home schedule with the Big Three.

A balanced home-away schedule was an objective of Dartmouth's president, John Sloan Dickey. Dartmouth, as an annual choice for TV network coverage, reaped financial rewards far beyond any other Ivy team. Another of President Dickey's creations was the revenue sharing system that gave every Ivy athletic program a piece of a very lucrative pie dominated by Dartmouth and the Big Three. Brown, Columbia, Cornell and Penn seldom, if ever, had TV dates in the 60s.

Dartmouth football coach Bob Blackman (right) is interviewed by Howard Cosell, the national sports commentator, during the program in New York City when Dartmouth was awarded the Lambert Trophy as the East's outstanding team following the Big Green's undefeated season in 1965. After another undefeated season and another Lambert Trophy in 1970, Blackman left Dartmouth with a record of 104-37-3 over 16 seasons to coach at Illinois.

While Dartmouth football has struggled in recent years, the Blackman years were truly golden years, never more memorably than when Penn State coach Joe Paterno challenged Blackman's undefeated team in 1970 to a playoff game. The Dartmouth coach had the last word: "Ivy League rules don't permit us to play a post-season game. But if we could, we'd prefer to play a team with a better record than Penn State (7-3)."

— Seaver Peters, Director of Athletics at Dartmouth, 1967-83

The expansion of Memorial Field's east grandstand in 1968 brought the stadium's seating capacity to 20,416. Over the next decade, Dartmouth played to several capacity crowds for games with Princeton, Harvard, Yale and Cornell. With the construction of Floren Varsity House in 2007, the east stands were reduced to 3,000 seats and the Memorial Field capacity to 13,000.

Both: Courtesy Dartmouth Athletic Department

Jon Gilbert Fox

Courtesy Dartmouth Athletic Department

Artificial surfaces reflect state-of-the-art improvements for Dartmouth's Memorial Field and Red Rolfe Field at Biondi Park. The football and baseball facilities flank Floren Varsity House (another addition in 2007). During past decade, Dartmouth invested about $80 million in construction and renovation of athletic facilities to serve student-athletes at all levels as well as others in the Dartmouth community. Below, Thompson Arena opened in 1975 as the home of Dartmouth hockey. It remains one of the nation's best intercollegiate ice facilities.

Dartmouth Life

As Dartmouth students walked across the Green early on a spring morning in 1968 they looked up to discover that time was being recorded by Mickey Mouse, installed during the night on the Baker Library clock by a couple of creative students who weren't afraid of height.

Coeducation arrived at Dartmouth in 1972 but not without occasional protest by male students who felt the College should remain an all-male institution.

During the late fall and winter of 1985-86, a group of Dartmouth students and faculty erected shanties on the Green to demonstrate their opposition to apartheid in South Africa. After four months students associated with the conservative Dartmouth Review peacefully dismantled the shanties. The group was arrested, without resistance, by campus police and subsequently suspended by a court consisting of faculty and students with apparent sympathy for the shanty builders.

There have been countless Dartmouth Winter Carnival sculptures on the Green. Two of the most memorable: The Statue of Liberty that recognized the national bicentennial in 1976 and, below, the fire-breathing dragon that was a highlight of Winter Carnival in 1969.

Few events bring town and gown together like the bonfire, built by members of the freshman class, on the center of the Green and set afire at the conclusion of a Friday night rally that attracts several thousand spectators during Dartmouth's annual homecoming football weekend. The freshmen follow an engineered plan to build the tiers with square timbers (replacing old railroad ties that were used for many years). Safety regulations now set the height of the bonfire at about 60 tiers.

Joseph Mehling

Dartmouth-Hitchcock Medical Center

On October 5, 1991, Dr. C. Everett Koop, a Dartmouth graduate (1937) and retired Surgeon General of the United States, led the ceremonial parade that accompanied the precision-like transfer of patients from old Mary Hitchcock Memorial Hospital to the new Dartmouth-Hitchcock Medical Center in Lebanon. Dr. Koop carried the medical bag that belonged to Dr. Nathan Smith, founder of Dartmouth Medical School in 1797. With Dr. Koop is Stevie Northrop, a patient at DHMC whose plastic box holds the saddlebags used by Dr. Smith when he made house calls.

The Medical Center Moves

The journey during the 1980s that led to the Dartmouth-Hitchcock Medical Center's move from Hanover to Lebanon was long, winding and bumpy. When it was complete and the new DHMC opened in 1991, the story (it's worthy of a book) proved to be a remarkable collaboration of flexible and creative leaders representing Hanover, Dartmouth College, the Medical Center, and the City of Lebanon who collectively put their heads together and found a solution.

During the 1960s and 70s, the Medical Center—Mary Hitchcock Memorial Hospital (MHMH), the Hitchcock Clinic (the doctors), Dartmouth Medical School (DMS)—was an evolving institution.

The hospital had about 400 beds with a growing trend toward specialty and outpatient treatment. DMS, for many years a two-year program, was heading toward a three- and then a four-year curriculum. Before the four-year program, DMC had a long-term affiliation with Brown University's medical school where a cohort of students spent the first two years at DMS and the last two years at Brown.

Hospital facilities on Maynard Street, north of the Dartmouth campus, were bulging. The only way to expand was up or north, beyond the medical school.

In 1982, a hospital-clinic expansion plan that involved a new facility on Dewey Field north of the medical school came before the Hanover Planning Board. After nearly two years of discussion that focused heavily on concerns over traffic and parking, in the fall of 1984 the Planning Board turned down the plan.

The Dartmouth-Hitchcock Medical Center in Lebanon.

Joseph Mehling

Nearly four years after the Medical Center moved from Hanover to Lebanon, Faulkner House, the principal building of the old Mary Hitchcock Memorial Hospital, was turned to rubble in a spectacular implosion on September 9, 1995.

If not at the location it had grown on over 90 years, where could the Medical Center go? Developing a second campus to complement the Maynard Streeet campus was considered but abandoned in favor of keeping all Medical Center activities together. Two separate sites to create an integrated DHMC campus entered the discussion—one entirely in Lebanon, the other straddling the Hanover-Lebanon town line but largely in Lebanon.

In 1981, Dartmouth had acquired the 2000-acre Landmark property with no specific plans for its use. Paul Paganucci, the vice president and chief financial advisor to Dartmouth's president, David McLaughlin, called it, "...akin to the purchase of Alaska by the United States."

The second site, the Gile Tract, was a parcel of nearly 290 acres that had been a gift to the Town of Hanover in the early 1950s. The buildable area of the tract was in Lebanon. Coincidentally, the College's Sachem Field property to the west abutted both the Gile and Landmark properties.

In the fall of 1985, senior officers of the Medical Center organizations engaged in increasingly serious negotiations regarding relocation of the Medical Center. By mid-November, they reached agreement on the basic terms of such a move. During the last six weeks of 1985, including holidays and Dartmouth's term break, they were able to:

• Obtain approvals by all the trustees of three DHMC organizations as well as the Dartmouth faculty that had concerns that a costly Medical Center move would have an adverse impact on their programs.

• Negotiate and sign a comprehensive agreement binding the parties to proceed with the Medical Center move.

• Sell $218 million in tax-exempt bonds to pay for the new facility—before the December 31, 1985 expiration of rules permitting such a financing.

Concurrently, two totally unrelated events were capturing local headlines and warrant mention: Through the winter, College investments in South Africa led to protests and campus unrest, visible with the construction of shanties on the Green. And, the College was heading toward a contentious lawsuit involving the firing of Joe Yukica, the football coach who wanted the College to honor his existing contract.

Discussions then continued through the winter of 1986 on which land would work best for the new Medical Center. In March 1986, the Hanover Board of Selectmen approved a swap: Dartmouth would get the Gile Tract as the Medical Center site. The Town would get a parcel at Sachem Field from the College for recreation use. The Town would also get a long-term conservation easement running through the Landmark property.

What all this meant for the Medical Center:

• The hospital and clinical faculty (doctors are members of the Dartmouth faculty) would move to the new campus in Lebanon. Some basic science faculty would remain in existing Medical School buildings on the north end of the Dartmouth campus while others would move to new DMS facilities at the new DHMC campus in Lebanon.

• Dartmouth would purchase the Maynard Street land and buildings from MHMH and work with DHMC in a major capital campaign.

• The Norris Cotton Cancer Center that had grown measurably during the 1980s would eventually also move to the new campus (it happened in 1995).

Construction for the "new" DHMC began in 1988. In a scenario that was executed with military precision, the facility began operation on October 5, 1991. Four years later, the old hospital came down in a spectacular implosion. Today, the site is occupied by a group of College dormitories.

With the opening of the new DHMC, the City of Lebanon became the location for one of New Hampshire's largest employers. Although the Medical Center remained a non-profit enterprise and therefore tax exempt, the city would receive from DHMC substantial payments in lieu of taxes to address municipal service and infrastructure requirements.

As one of the participants in the Medical Center's move observed, "This project reflects the evolution of regionalization and cooperation. It has allowed Hanover to remain a distinctive New England town. And, the ability for DHMC to grow has had an obvious influence on the regional economy." *(J.D.)*

Fifteen years later: By 2010, the site of the old Medical Center along Maynard Street had become the north campus of Dartmouth College. Moving clockwise from left side of the parking lot: The original yellow brick hospital building, with its distinctive roof that dates from 1893, now houses offices of Dartmouth Medical School. The main DMS academic buildings are at the top of photo. Adjacent to the right is the McLaughlin Cluster of undergraduate dormitories. In the right foreground is Moore Hall, home of Dartmouth's psychology department.

Jon Gilbert Fox

The Time Capsule

No one knew what the tiny box contained. It was copper—about five inches square and two inches deep. The serendipitous find occurred after the 1995 implosion of Mary Hitchcock's Faulkner Building when workmen were moving the original Mary Hitchcock Memorial Hospital cornerstone to reposition it. They noticed that a pocket had been cut out of the top of the cornerstone and a piece of slate had been affixed as a cover. When they removed the slate, they discovered the box.

Curiosity about its contents grew as word spread. In a ceremony, with hundreds of staff and friends gathered in the main rotunda of DHMC, I had the privilege, with my predecessor, Bill Wilson (who served from 1948-1978), to open the metal box that had become known as the time capsule. It was filled with plans and artifacts with an envelope prominently placed on top of its contents. In that envelope was a handwritten letter from Hiram Hitchcock, benefactor and founder of the hospital he built in memory of his wife, Mary Maynard Hitchcock. With great excitement and anticipation I read the letter to the group:

"This box is, this seventeenth day of July 1890, placed in the corner stone of the Mary Hitchcock Memorial Hospital at Hanover, NH. This hospital, at the time of its completion in 1891, will perhaps be the most perfect of its kind then in existence. It is a memorial of one of the noblest and best of God's gifts to the Human race. God grant that this Hospital may be all, and more than all, that she would have it to be. She was my life here. May God in his infinite mercy unite us again."

It was an emotional and magical moment that no one in attendance will ever forget. The link to our past became tangible. I hope we always remember the expectations, dreams and love Hiram Hitchcock expressed for the future of our medical center.

(The opening of the 1890 Mary Hitchcock time capsule took place on October 5, 1995, the fourth anniversary of the Dartmouth-Hitchcock Medical Center move to Lebanon's new campus on October 5, 1991.)

— James W. Varnum, President, Mary Hitchcock Memorial Hospital, 1978-2006

In a ceremony in the rotunda of the new Medical Center in October 2005, Jim Varnum, president of Mary Hitchcock Memorial Hospital, reads the letter, written by Hiram Hitchcock in 1890, that was preserved in a copper box in the cornerstone of the original hospital.

Public Education

Out of a Sleepless Night...

For the better part of a decade beginning in the early 90s, the Dresden School Board wrestled with options for improving and expanding the Richmond Middle School and Hanover High School facilities, including a new location for additional athletics fields. Multiple generations of the School Board and community task forces explored many options, most with frighteningly high price tags. The Board of Selectmen and Town staff was reeled in from time to time. Things looked bleak as option after option was either withdrawn or shot down by the community.

Then, in early 2003, Brian Walsh, chair of the Board of Selectmen, was having another sleepless night. For several years he had pondered the quandary of Dresden facilities. As he tossed and turned, Brian found himself focusing on a potential solution to the school facilities problem. Brian spent most of the night hatching an ingenious plan for a complex series of property swaps and financial contributions involving the Town, the School District and Dartmouth College.

The next morning he called me and outlined his plan. Literally overnight, I inherited an exciting and all-consuming project. My job as Town Manager was to assist Brian in fleshing out and then quietly exploring the feasibility with several community leaders including School Board members and Dartmouth College staff. What began as a diagram on a piece of paper, sketched in the early morning hours, became a complex three-party negotiation ultimately leading to the "Three Party Agreement."

Julia Griffin has been Hanover's Town Manager since 1996.

Approved by voters at the Dresden School Meeting in March 2004 and at Town Meeting two months later, the "Agreement" resulted in the construction of a new Richmond Middle School (constructed on land donated by Dartmouth College), the expansion and renovation of Hanover High School, a substantial reconfiguration and expansion of the District's athletics fields, and a commitment of funds to assist in the project from Dartmouth and the Town.

— *Julia Griffin*

Before he became a business and community leader in Hanover, Brian Walsh was an outstanding lacrosse goaltender. The 1965 Dartmouth graduate was airborne as he made a save against Harvard in 1964. As he recalled, "I made the save but we lost the game." Walsh was the All-Ivy League goaltender in 1964 and 1965 and Dartmouth was the Ivy League co-champion in both seasons.

Hanover High School

The governance of Hanover High School changed in November 1963 when federal legislation confirmed the Articles of Agreement to form the Dresden School District comprising the schools of both Hanover and Norwich, Vt.

This legislation was among the last bills signed by President John F. Kennedy before his departure to Dallas and his untimely death on November 22. With Norwich and Hanover joining hands in the new school district, Hanover High was on its way to becoming a modern, all-inclusive school.

Hanover High became one of the nation's first public schools to participate in A Better Chance (ABC), a program that offered educational opportunity to minority high school students. Among those who came to Hanover High was Jesse Spikes.

The son, and youngest of 13 children, of a Georgia sharecropper, Spikes came to Hanover in 1966 at age 16 and lived with Lou and Peter Gardner (Pete was Dartmouth's crew coach). From Hanover High, Spikes graduated from Dartmouth in 1972. He went on to Oxford as a Rhodes Scholar and then graduated from Harvard Law School. Today, he is a prominent lawyer in Atlanta.

With the arrival of Arthur Pierce (the second superintendent here with that name) and Roland Miller as principal in 1968 and the issuing of the Kreider Report challenging Hanover High to improve its total program, the school began a transformation. An "open concept" organization allowed students the freedom to leave school if they didn't have a regularly scheduled class. This concept remains in effect today—witness the many students crossing Lebanon and Park streets to shop for lunch at the Hanover Co-op.

A second major change in the high school, in 1971, was the creation of a new "Council," that replaced the traditional student council. This new organization included elected students, faculty and townspeople. The Council has the authority to set policy and to govern the student body in a democratic fashion.

The high school building opened on Lebanon Street in 1935 (HHS had been on Allen Street since 1913) and was enlarged in the late 60s to provide for better learning and library space. With the opening of the new elementary school in 1970, high school and junior high students were separated into two buildings: The junior high students took over the former elementary classroom space.

From 1983 until he departed in 2001 to become headmaster of the American Embassy School in India (where he had taught 20 years earlier), Hanover High grew under the leadership of Uwe Bagnato, a strong and compassionate advocate for his students.

In the early years of the past decade, schools were (as always) the topic of conversation in Hanover and Norwich. With the final decision to move the Richmond Middle School to Lyme Road, the high school underwent a major renovation and expansion. The new atrium, cafeteria, gymnasium and library are but a few of the improvements to the facility. Outdoors, the addition of an artificial turf field has added a new dimension to Hanover High athletics.

One of the school's curricular innovations is March Intensive, a four-day program that enriches the academic experience. All regular classes are suspended and students select an activity of their choice. Examples: building a new computer or skate board, studying French impressionist art, trips to build a Habitat for Humanity House in Florida or traveling with the Wind Ensemble for a series of concerts in Germany.

Hanover High School continues to rank among the outstanding schools in New Hampshire (public and private), producing top-ranked students who thrive as they experience the benefits of a comprehensive curriculum. *(W.B.)*

Recent renovations at Hanover High reflect an airy, open atmosphere.

Fifty Years at Hanover High

When I arrived at Hanover High School in the fall of 1961, the male teachers wore coats and ties and an occasional suit. Women, whether adults or students, were seldom seen in slacks. Sometimes a female student could convince the administration that it was all right to wear slacks because they were helping with the Ford Sayre ski program after school.

We ate tray lunches in a staff or student cafeteria during a real lunch period in the middle of a seven-period day. The curriculum was generally the same for all, built around an English 9-10-11-12 program. The students were divided into four academic sections depending largely on their English section. If you were in Section One for English, you were likely to be in section one for math and science. The sections were frequently criticized for representing parents' backgrounds as much as academic skills.

Bill Murphy has seen, and helped to shape, innumerable changes since he arrived at Hanover High two months after Hanover celebrated its bicentennial in 1961.

In order to get my teaching contract, I was expected to sign a loyalty oath that I was not a member of the Communist Party and that I would not advocate the violent overthrow of the government. I was paid the princely sum of $4,200 as a beginning teacher with a Master's degree. Because I was married, part of this salary included a head of household stipend that was not paid to women. Teachers were paid once a month, and I can remember visiting in-laws for meals on weekends at the end of the month and before the next pay check arrived. I earned an additional $300 for coaching varsity boys' basketball and jayvee baseball. We included Enfield, Orford, Charlestown, and Woodsville on our basketball schedule, probably commensurate with our abilities since there was no organized basketball program in Hanover below ninth grade. Bookkeeping was not as strict as today; I would simply walk into the basement of Campion's on Main Street to buy what I needed for the team, and have them send a bill to the school.

I've taught through at least three renovations and the relocation of the elementary and junior high schools from Lebanon Street to their new sites as the Ray and Richmond schools. I was there when the Dresden School District was created as the first interstate school district in the nation when President Kennedy signed the enabling resolution before going on to Dallas in 1963.

I survived the educational revolution of the late 1960s and early 70s when we eliminated grades, study halls and the dress code, opened the campus, emphasized electives in a mod schedule that at one time included 21 mods in a school day. We were the target of a Manchester Union Leader expose and labeled "Bedlam City." We initiated a movement towards a more democratic school that culminated in our current Council that is a model for many other schools. No other educational reform movement has come close to matching that period 40 years ago, but over time we have returned to a rather traditional curriculum in a rather liberal social setting.

A constant in this 50-year period: The students, who remain the vital force in the school. They still treat getting their drivers licenses as a rite of passage. They still grow over the year in understanding what is expected of a research paper. They still have dances, but not in the old auditorium where parents were known to view the prom from the balcony. They still seek championships in athletics to add to the banners in the gymnasium. They still worry about grades, college applications and getting into a good college. The students I teach are still 16 years of age, and this leads me to believe that I have found the fountain of youth, for if they are still 16, I must still be 23.

— *Bill Murphy, 1987 New Hampshire Teacher of the Year*

Quiz Bowl

Question: "What Hanover High School team actually won state championships in both Vermont and New Hampshire in the same year?"

If you answered the Quiz Bowl team, you would be right. By virtue of being an interstate school district, Hanover High students have competed in both states for over 20 years: the New Hampshire Quiz Bowl League, the Granite State Challenge that airs on New Hampshire Public Television, and the Vermont Scholars Bowl. Any student can compete in the weekly practices and the regional tournaments and the very best go on to the state championship rounds where Hanover has done very well, winning several times. The team won all three events in 2003.

The Granite State Challenge in 2010 was one of the most exciting finals ever held. Competing with two subs, Hanover lost in overtime to Manchester Central. Our team captain and another regular didn't compete due to a conflict: They were in the cast of the annual school play.

— *Bill Murphy, founder and coach of the HHS Quiz Bowl Team*

Hanover High March Intensive

Diversity is a word that describes student interests at Hanover High, especially during the innovative four-day March Intensive Program, introduced in 2008, that offers more than 50 learning experiences that differ from the school's regular curriculum offerings.

All: Jon Gilbert Fox

Class Ties

It was spring of 1951 and the 52 members of our Hanover High School class looked forward to graduation and the future. Three of us had made plans for the military, 24 for college, and 25 to work in New England. Our teachers tried to impart their zest for learning and challenged us as we headed into the unknown. Our graduation speaker, John H. Hines, implored our class "to be alert to the problems of education so that we can have the schools that are so vital to a thriving democracy."

Our class has held a reunion every five years. Early ones were held at Storrs Pond, then at the Holiday Inn and the Norwich Inn, before settling on Pierce's Inn in Etna. We've "lost" classmates but thanks to letters in the Valley News we found one. Another wrote, "I ain't lost, I work the night shift at Goodyear Tire in Windsor." Other "missing" classmates have been found through old friends, college classmates, and the helpful postmistress of a small Colorado town who recognized the name of a classmate—she was living in a trailer on a friend's property.

At our 50th reunion in 2001 we reveled in our classmates' broad interests and activities. Teachers and professors led the way in careers. Others included engineers, truck drivers, lawyers, building contractors, doctors, foresters, an airline pilot and a number in business. Favorite teachers were remembered, politics was STILL debated, just as we did in history and social studies classes. Sporting events were reviewed "as if yesterday" and we wondered what happened to those "old jalopies."

For our 60th reunion, to be held during Hanover's 250th celebration, we look forward to renewing friendships. We now have 37 classmates from Canada and across the USA. Forrie Branch, the coach and one of our social studies teachers, told us, "Play the game from the first down to the last." We're still together after all these years.

— *Nancy Hayward Mitchell, HHS 1951*

Analog...Digital

Whitey Burnham, a coach (soccer, lacrosse, wrestling) and athletic administrator at Dartmouth for nearly 30 years, didn't throw things away. After Whitey and Joanne (they were long-time bridge partners with my parents), died recently, their daughter, Janice, was clearing their home and sent me a copy of a Hanover phone book from 1960, the year the Burnhams came to Hanover.

The conversion to dial telephones happened in 1961. Before that, our number, after being asked by the local operator, "Number, please…," was 1058. We were among those fortunate to have a private line. Many of my friends had a shared, two-party line, denoted by three digits followed by either M or R. M and R families tended to know a lot about each other. Hanover and surrounding towns had to be one of the last areas of the United States to get dial telephones. It was also about the same time, as I was entering Hanover High, that Hanover got its first traffic lights. Talk about progress…

As this was happening, a young math professor at Dartmouth, John Kemeny, was turning all things analog to digital. Due to his influence as a member of the school board, Hanover High was perhaps the first high school to teach BASIC and have a computer terminal in the building. Since there was only one terminal, there was always a waiting line to use it. As a sophomore, I remember sneaking into College Hall (now Collis) to try out my program that could count backward from 100 to zero by 5s and print the result. It worked! I was a geek.

— *Bill Wilson, HHS '66, Dartmouth '70*

The Class of 1973

Graduation day for Hanover High School's Class of 1973 dawned clear and cool. The seniors performed well at the morning's graduation rehearsal and now, as the early evening event began, they filed onto the stage of the Bema. They endured the exhortations and celebratory speeches well, all the while waiting eagerly for the big moment: the awarding of their diplomas.

As principal, I stood behind a small podium and prepared to read the names of each graduate. Upon hearing his or her name, each graduate walked across the front of the stage to receive the diploma and congratulations from the chairperson of the School Board and return, basking in the applause of family and friends. I read the first name. Then everything fell apart.

The first graduate received her diploma but, instead of directly returning to her seat, she walked over to me with her hand outstretched. How nice, I thought, she wants to shake my hand. Well, the graduate did shake my hand, but also placed a small round object in it. She grinned and walked back to her seat. I quickly glanced down and saw that she had given me a marble.

One hundred and fifty four marbles followed that first one. Marbles were bulging from all pockets of my suit, rolling off the podium and onto and off the stage, all to the general mirth of the graduates behind me and the bewilderment of parents and friends trying to see what was happening.

When the last diploma was awarded, I changed the traditional line, "Ladies and gentlemen I present to you the Class of 1973", to "Ladies and gentlemen, you have just witnessed the Class of 1973 lose their marbles!"

The next morning, still smiling about the gentle prank of the previous night's graduates, I opened my office door to be confronted with, wall to wall and floor to ceiling helium-inflated balloons! The Class of 1974 was serving notice!

— *Robert McCarthy, Principal, Hanover High School, 1971-1980*

Hanover High Athletics

Hanover High School's teams have enjoyed success longer than the past 50 years. Under the guidance of numerous outstanding coaches including Forrie Branch, Dot Merriman, George Merrill, Chuck Hunnewell, Mike Ivanoski, the Dodds brothers (Dick and John), Jim Eakin, Jean Essex, Dan O'Rourke and Mike Jackson, the achievements of countless Marauder athletes dot the championship ledger of the New Hampshire Interscholastic Athletic Association (NHIAA).

Forrest (Forrie) Branch graduated from Dartmouth in 1933 and arrived at Hanover High in 1937. Over the next 39 years, Forrie became a legendary coach, teacher, athletics director and mentor for thousands of Hanover students. Among his associates was Dot Merriman. From 1955-82, Dot had many outstanding field hockey teams and built the foundation for girls' athletics at Hanover High.

Over the past 50 years, Hanover High athletes have enjoyed success on fields, in the gym and ice rinks, and on the ski slopes, winning over 180 state championships in their division. State titles have been won in nearly every sport offered at HHS.

Hanover has dominated in skiing events with the boys winning 31 state titles. The girls are close behind with 30 state titles. For proof that Hanover kids enjoy running: The girls have captured 13 team titles in cross country while the boys have nine titles.

While football won two Division IV titles in the 60s and three more in the past decade, soccer has been Hanover's most successful fall sport. The boys have earned 18 state titles

Football and other teams benefit from the artificial turf at the new Forrie Branch Field that was created as part of the recent Hanover High expansion and renovation.

including the past six in Class I competition. The girls have won six championships. In the spring season, Hanover has won 12 titles in tennis (10 for the boys, two for the girls).

On the ice, the boys have won eight Division One titles. In one of Hanover's newest offerings (since 2008), the Marauder girls have captured three state titles. Hanover boys enjoy hitting the ball or puck, as they have also won 11 state titles in tennis.

But, do you know the sport that enjoys the greatest participation among HHS students? It's rowing, a program established during the 90s for the girls with rowing for boys added in recent years. No other Hanover High sport finds its student-athletes getting out of bed before sunrise to train on the Connecticut River. *(W.B.)*

Rowing is the highest participation sport at Hanover High. It began in the 90s as a girls' sport but now includes boys crew as well.

Hanover High Champions

Tiger Shaw

During the past decade, the Hanover High girls' soccer team won five state titles, most recently in 2008.

Dick Dodds began coaching the Hanover High boys hockey team in 1982. In January 2011 the Marauder skaters presented him with his 400th career coaching victory.

Alan MacRae

The Hanover High boys soccer team celebrated its sixth straight state championship in 2010 and 17th in NHIAA competition over the past 40 years.

Courtesy: Dick Dodds

Courtesy: John Dodds

Girls' hockey became a NHIAA championship sport in 2008. In 2011, the Hanover High skaters, coached by John Dodds (Dick's brother), won their third state title in four years.

The Ski Jumper

It's February 1961 and I'm standing at the top of the 45-meter jump, the 90-foot towering steel structure in the Vale of Tempe at Hanover Country Club. I'm looking out across the fairways, with ticket booths set up for the hundreds of people streaming in to join the thousands already lining the out-run of the jump.

The parking lots at the old Garipay farm off Reservoir Road are overflowing. I can see students and their dates walking out Lyme Road and across the 15th fairway. This is the Big Event, the culmination of the Dartmouth Winter Carnival.

I'm 11 years old and this is my first invitation to fore jump before the collegiate competition begins.

Time to fly. I push off and plunge down the icy track, skis rattling, wind whistling as I go faster and faster—10, 20, 30 miles per hour toward the takeoff. Leaping forward into the air, the sounds have suddenly disappeared. I'm clawing at the air. My speed overcomes gravity for a few seconds. Will I be able to land on the steep, hard landing area with a telemark, just as my coaches had trained me?

Gravity finally wins. With an awkward squat I return to earth, zooming through the transition to the outrun. I suddenly notice the crowds—yelling and clapping in tribute to the kid that made it. This is the excitement and fun that ski jumping is all about.

Hanover and Norwich had many jumps back then, from small handmade hills scattered in farm fields (where most kids started) to Sample's 20-meter hill in Norwich. There was a 30-meter hill on the slope to the north of the fifth fairway and green at the golf course (it's now grown to woods). This was one of the first hills to have plastic beads that allowed summer jumping—but you had to carry bags of beads back up to replenish the supply on the hill.

The 90-foot steel tower beside the 15th fairway was the "big 45-meter hill" that was first used in 1922 (and torn down in the 1980s). Every kid growing up in Hanover dreamed about jumping this hill in front of the huge crowds. The Dartmouth Carnival was a major event with college jumpers battling for the title. On top of this we all heard bizarre stories of college students coming down the jump on skis, sleds and others means, often ending in injury and disaster.

Dreams became reality for many kids from the Hanover area (more than

anywhere else in the USA) representing the United States in the Olympics, World Cup and national jumping competition.

The NCAA Ski Committee made a terrible decision by eliminating jumping in 1977, bringing an end to a long tradition of collegiate jumping. Yet jumping in Hanover continues today. In 1972, the Ford Sayre ski program built 20- and 30-meter hills at Oak Hill in the Storrs Pond recreation area. This allowed area boys and girls to enjoy ski jumping lessons. They formed the backbone of the Hanover High jumping program. Hanover High has won more state championships than any other high school in New Hampshire. While the rest of the country went to club jumping after the NCAA decision, New Hampshire is the only state in the nation that still has ski jumping as an interscholastic sport.

Ski Jumping has always captured the imagination of kids to fly. For many decades it was the only means of achieving non-mechanical flight for a few seconds. Now there are all sorts of big air competitions with snowboards, X-Games and freestyle. But ski jumping in Hanover is a tradition that carries on.

— *Bruce (Buff) McLaughry*

The Vale of Tempe ski jump at Hanover Country Club was torn down in the 1980s. When Buff McLaughry was a youthful fore jumper in the early 1960s the intercollegiate jumping competition was a highlight of Dartmouth's Winter Carnival.

Adrian Bouchard

Richmond Middle School

In 1970, when the Ray School opened, the former elementary school building that was built in 1932 became Hanover's middle school, housing grades 5-8. In 1971, the students voted to name the school in honor of their former elementary school librarian, Frances Richmond. In 1973 the fifth grade was moved to the Ray School, creating a sixth- through eighth-grade middle school.

The school received two National Excellence in Education Awards, one in 1988-89 and another in 1998-99. Susan Finer, then principal, journeyed to Washington to accept the awards on behalf of her school.

With the RMS and HHS becoming overcrowded, it was voted to move the Richmond School to its current site on Lyme Road (it opened in 2005). It took hours of discussion and planning and many school meeting votes before a plan was approved to build the new middle school and renovate the high school. *(W.B.)*

Courtesy of Richmond School

Susan Finer was principal of the Richmond Middle School from 1985 until she retired in 2007. Under her leadership the school won two National Excellence in Education Awards.

Jon Gilbert Fox

The new Richmond Middle School opened on Lyme Road in 2005.

The Ray School

Hanover's new elementary school opened on the Reservoir Road site in September 1970. Originally housing the kindergarten through fourth grade, after several years the fifth grade was added. Named for Bernice A. Ray, the long-time principal of the Hanover Elementary School, the building was designed for "open classroom learning" complete with pods of classrooms and sliding doors between the rooms. Sited in a natural setting, the grounds included hills, hemlock forests, a winding stream, a pond, and open fields. It was a perfect location for the environmental education of young students.

In 1976, as the Town's national bicentennial project, a replica of a 200-year old colonial house was built. The students helped raise money, cleaned the bricks for the fireplace, and studied colonial life to ensure the building's authenticity. To this day, the second grade celebrates "Colonial Day" at the house, and every Thanksgiving the entire school visits the house, classroom by classroom, to revisit history, and swap tales and ideas.

One feature missing from the original school was an adequate playground. In 1984, a group of parents began fund raising and planning for a new recreation structure. They chose Robert Leathers to be the architect. On an October weekend in 1985, 1,341 volunteers assembled to construct Playspace! It was an immediate success with students and townspeople.

In 1989, Emile Birch of Canaan was the artist-in-residence at the school. He guided students through the design and construction phases of a sculpture that became known as Facespace, now the symbol of the school.

Over the years, the Ray School has built traditions in every grade—the third grade Japanese Festival, the second grade Colonial Day, the fifth grade Medieval Festival, the all-school tumbling show, and the annual winter and spring musical concerts. Today, the school echoes with a zest for learning and a curiosity for the world about it. *(W.B.)*

A second grade class in 1978 celebrates "Colonial Day" at the replica colonial house that was built at the Ray School as the Town's national bicentennial project in 1976.

Courtesy of Ray School

The Facespace sculpture, created in 1989, is now the symbol of the Ray School.

Courtesy of Ray School

Though it was replaced after a decade of use, the Ray School's original Playspace, erected by over 1,300 volunteers in 1985, was a symbol of team effort by students and townspeople.

Anne Chapman Mellor

The "Tenured" Substitute

I began my life in Hanover as a stay-at-home mom but, with both daughters happily enrolled in the Hanover Elementary School, I found that I had time on my hands. The solution was simple; in 1969, I put my name on the Hanover school's substitute list.

Within a week, I was called. The query, "Would I be able to fill in for a couple of weeks for a kindergarten teacher who had broken her ankle?" "Sure," I said. The next day found me at the school facing 20 five-year-olds. Kindergarten was fun and, lo and behold, the teacher never returned so I stayed the whole year! There was a teacher vacancy in kindergarten the next fall, so I was hooked. I went from being a substitute to a full-time teacher.

Seven years later, the art teacher at the Ray School was taking a year off. I asked if I could substitute in art for the year. I did and you guessed it; the art teacher never returned. I stayed in the art room until I retired in 1992. You might categorize me as the longest tenured sub in Ray School history!

As my kids left home, again I had time on my hands. So, in 1981, I threw my hat in the ring to become a selectman. Little did I know that I would sit on the board for 21 years and then serve as Town Meeting moderator for another seven years.

As a selectman, I can truthfully report that I shared in two decisions that changed the life of Hanover. Those decisions were 1) to hire Cliff Vermilya as town manager, and 2) to hire Julia Griffin to succeed Cliff as manager. Cliff and Julia brought professionalism to the town that has moved us forward in a caring, thoughtful, fiscally sound manner.

My biggest blunder as selectman came the first time CATV came to videotape our meeting. It was a very hot summer evening and, forgetting the TV camera, I slipped out of my shoes. The cameraman focused on my bare feet and forgot to tape the meeting!

I've been privileged to work with Hanover's amazing children who made each day special at the Ray School. It was with the support of many talented colleagues that I was able to achieve my success.

Working with town government over the years has also been an honor. The employees of the town of Hanover are skilled, able to perform at a top level and always keep the citizens foremost in the planning and execution of their daily jobs. Their expertise makes the role of an elected official an easy task.

— *Marilyn (Willy) Black*

Since arriving in Hanover in the late 1960s, Marilyn (Willy) Black has had an unparalleled career as a kindergarten and art teacher at the Ray School, a member of the Board of Selectmen, the Town Meeting moderator, and a member of too many town and community committees to count.

At the White House in 1979, President Jimmy Carter honored Willy Black as the National Teacher of the Year. She remains the only teacher from New Hampshire to receive the award. In 1980, Dartmouth College added further recognition, presenting Willy with an honorary degree, Doctor of Humane Letters.

Lillian Bailey

My earliest memories of Lillian Bailey are from the Etna School that I attended from 1949 to 1953. There were two classrooms with four grades. I don't know if Mrs. Bailey was the principal, the head teacher or just the third and fourth grade teacher, but there was no question that she was in charge. And, she was always "Mrs. Bailey." It never dawned on me that she had a first name.

Certainly there was someone watching over us from higher up in the school system and there were teachers who came from outside regularly to teach music and penmanship. As I remember, we were pretty much self-contained. There was no hot lunch program, but once a week during the winter mothers would take turns bringing in hot soup.

Lillian Bailey's influence reached to all corners of the Hanover community.

At one point Mrs. Bailey had us set up a store in the basement of the school where students could take turns being store keeper and selling penny candy and inexpensive school supplies to the other students. This was her way of teaching us practical mathematics and commerce. We were allowed to go to the Etna Store during lunch to buy a snack but we had to ask correctly. If we said, "Can I go to the store?" she would answer that she was sure we were capable of it but it was necessary to say, "May I..."

A couple of years later Mrs. Bailey moved to the Hanover Elementary School where she taught my sixth grade class. (The Etna School closed in 1957. It's now the Etna post office.) She later taught third grade at the elementary school and, from 1966 until she retired in 1985 she was the reading specialist at the high school. She started the reading lab that is now named in her honor. She was always an enthusiastic teacher who genuinely cared about the children she taught.

After she retired from teaching, Mrs. Bailey worked part-time in the children's department at the Dartmouth Bookstore that was owned by my family for many years. Even then, she never stopped teaching many of Hanover's children.

— Ann Cioffi

School Nurses

Being a school nurse is an education. I was the Ray School nurse from 1988 until 2004, succeeding Jane Graham who became Hanover's third K-12 nurse in 1966 and moved to the Ray School when it opened in 1971.

There were times of great professional satisfaction, many joys and many challenges, moments that were humorous and heart wrenching. When I came to school nursing, the practice had evolved from one with a primary goal to reduce absenteeism due to communicable diseases to one with the emphasis on student wellness, disease prevention and health education.

A serendipitous meeting with Dr. C. Everett Koop in the early 90s led to a collaboration between the Koop Institute and local pre- and public schools. The Ray School played a leadership role in the planning of this collaboration. One of Dr. Koop's goals was to help medical students feel at ease and be effective in talking with children and adolescents about health issues. This partnership gave medical students and teachers a chance to work together in teaching health.

It also gave teachers an opportunity to learn health-teaching techniques taught by trained health educators and brought research-based health education concepts to the schools. Teachers and students from the Hanover, Lebanon, Claremont, Mascoma and South Royalton school districts participated in this initiative.

Fall and spring seemed to be times when head lice could wreak daily havoc in the classroom. Trying to be vigilant to these critters, I made frequent trips to classrooms. One day as I walked into a K-1 room, I heard a little voice say, "Oh, no, here she comes again, looking for 'headlights.'"

On another day, a teacher brought a student to me in frustration. This child had spent far too much time in the bathroom and the teacher wanted me to check him out. A simple question to the child brought the response, "I was just waiting until math was over."

There were times, too, when we pulled together as a school for grieving students and families and then, as a nation, on September 11, 2001. For me, the Ray School is a community in the true sense of the word, where cherished and enduring memories and friendships are formed, every day and at every level.

— Ann Bradley

Jon Gilbert Fox

Since the mid-1960s, the area along Reservoir Road (angling from top left) has grown steadily from farmland into a vibrant business-residential area. Through it all, the hub has been the Ray School (lower right), which opened in 1970.

This Special Community

Welcome to Hanover

Barrett Collection

The first bridge spanning the Connecticut River between Hanover and Norwich, Vt., was built in 1796. There were four replacements before the steel and concrete Ledyard Bridge (above) was completed in 1935. By the mid-1990s the volume of vehicular traffic had overwhelmed the 60-year old bridge leading to its replacement with the wider, two-pier bridge with its ornamental concrete globes that prompted controversy and conversation that has subsided since the bridge opened in 1999.

Courtesy Town of Hanover

Howe Library

As services and patrons at Howe Library steadily increased, November 1972 proved the turning point. The Howe had operated independently at its location in Emily Howe's old house on West Wheelock Street. Since its inception, Howe had asked the Town for a modest appropriation each year to help support operations.

At a League of Women Voters public meeting, Harry Bird, a member of Hanover's Finance Committee, suggested the Town should be asked to take over the entire operating budget of the library, beginning in 1973, if the Library used its endowment to build a new, expanded library.

In January 1973, the Corporation of the Library voted to put an article on the warrant for Town Meeting requesting the Town's total support of the operating budget. The article passed unanimously. Led by Posey Fowler, planning moved forward to build an up-to-date facility.

Groundbreaking ceremonies for the new Library were held on Nov 4, 1974. Honorary Mayor Harry Tanzi presided, assisted by Mrs. Fowler, Lou Bressett and Edward Brown (representing the Town), and Dartmouth President John Kemeny.

The new Howe opened on East South Street in December 1975. Patti Eckels, the librarian, with Posey Fowler, had orchestrated the fund raising and construction of the building. It was a moment of pride for the town and the library board.

The library celebrated its 100th birthday, with a parade on September 17, 1999. Portraying Emily Howe and her husband, Hiram Hitchcock, were Priscilla Weisman and Leonard Morrissey, Jr.

In 2003, with yet more users and the need for a wider collection of materials, the library was again cramped for space. Posey Fowler returned to action and, with Ralph Manuel as her co-chair, plans for another expansion were soon under way. On October 25, 2005, the expanded Howe Library was complete. With the Town supporting operations, the Howe Corporation raised funds for the addition—at no additional cost to the taxpayers. *(W.B.)*

Adrian Bouchard

From 1900 to 1975, Howe Library was located in the renovated house on West Wheelock Street that, before relocation from the Dartmouth campus in 1838, was the original home of Eleazar Wheelock, Dartmouth's first president.

Courtesy: Howe Library

Joan (Posey) Fowler (center) reviews drawings with Charlie Judd (left) Trumbull-Nelson's site superintendent and Fred White, president of Dartmouth National Bank, during construction of Howe Library in 1974. Fowler was a leading member of the committee that planned for the new library as well as the library's expansion 30 years later.

Hanover students make the Howe Library lounge an active after-school study site.

Jon Gilbert Fox

Howe Memories

About the Howe Library: I have memories of two very different women to share.

One was an elderly woman, who shall be nameless. She came in one morning, circa 1970, when we were still in the old Wheelock house, now Roberts Flowers, and found me happily transferring the LP vinyl record collection from orange crates where they'd resided to a handsome new record storage bin.

This was such an improvement! Now you could see the fronts of the covers. I asked her how she liked the new record bin. She sniffed grumpily, "Well, it's not very COLONIAL." She was probably not the only elderly person in town who suspected the library was now being run by a rather young woman from California, of all places, who was going to change the way things had always been done in this quiet New England town. Forty years ago Hanover was, indeed, a relatively quiet town— no interstates nearby, no year-round college operation, no huge medical center.

At opening day of Howe Library on December 8, 1975, Librarian Patricia Eckels checks out the first book to Dorothy Hurlbutt who was the Howe's librarian from 1952-65.

The other elderly woman was Margaret McCallum. Mrs. McCallum had long been a trustee of the library and once joked that she'd represented Howe at so many functions she feared people would confuse her with Emily Howe. Shortly after we moved to Hanover in 1966 she invited me to tea to talk about whether I might be interested in the position of Head Librarian at Howe. And, of course, to look me over. Everyone in town knew Margaret. She wrote a weekly column for the Hanover Gazette, wrote short blurbs in the fronts of new library books, signing them MBMcC, and was an accomplished and thoroughly delightful woman.

When I came on board at Howe I was astonished to find that the Librarian attended trustee meetings, only when "invited." I expressed to Mrs. McCallum my dismay at trying to run a library with so little communication between trustees and Librarian. Two months later I found a note on my desk from Margaret: The Trustees had decided the Librarian should be present at all meetings. Not for the first time, or the last, she used her powers of gentle persuasion and quiet diplomacy to solve a community problem.

— *Patricia Wood (Patti) Eckels, Librarian, 1967-87*

Facing page: A dramatic nighttime view of the Howe Library after the library was expanded in 2005.

The Howe Library is a resource for reading and research.

A Double Life

A chance encounter 43 years ago on a trans-Atlantic ocean liner led my family to Hanover where we've been fortunate to have an exciting professional life while also participating in the civic life of the town.

In 1969, I became a research assistant and electron microscopist at Dartmouth Medical School. Over the subsequent 40 years DMS grew, as did Dartmouth College with the arrival of coeducation. The Dartmouth-Hitchcock Medical Center emerged as a unifying entity that combined Mary Hitchcock Hospital, the Hitchcock Clinic, the Medical School and the Norris Cotton Cancer Center. DHMC became an ever-enlarging research and primary care institution, leading to its move from Hanover to Lebanon in 1991.

Midway through a satisfying professional career I found myself working at two locations. My equipment and laboratory was at DMS in Hanover while the department for which I did clinical pathology was in Lebanon. A system emerged that allowed me to work on both campuses until I retired in 2008.

My double life began in the 1980s. Our home is in the juxta-downtown area where we observed first hand the pressures of accommodating the municipal parking problems as well as off-campus undergraduate student housing. Being named to the Zoning Board of Adjustment in the early 80s allowed me to gain a broad knowledge of the town and its citizens while working with fellow citizen board members. I began to realize the unique effectiveness of Hanover's citizen government participation. In 1988, I was elected to the Board of Selectmen where I remain to this day.

I've served on the Board of Selectmen with an amazing group of men and women who brought diverse talents and bodies of knowledge to the service of our citizens. I've participated in a system that allows for efficient and well-functioning Town services by dedicated and long-serving employees.

I've been truly proud to participate in enabling the building of the Public Works garage, the municipal parking facility, the Howe Library addition, the Richard W. Black Center and the municipalization of the Hanover Water Company, all outstanding facilities that enjoy record-breaking use or simply happy customers.

I have also proudly participated in the ceremonies that joined Hanover with our Friendship Cities—Joigny, France and Nihonmatsu, Japan—relationships that are active to this day.

So, thank you, Benning Wentworth, for granting Hanover's charter that created the town so many have built upon over the past 250 years and where it's been my privilege to participate in exciting parallel lives for the last 40 years.

— *Kate Connolly*

Kate Connolly has served on numerous Town committees, including the Board of Selectmen, since the 1980s.

Jon Gilbert Fox

Love at First Sight

The first time I drove up the hill to Hanover it was love at first sight. I knew in an instant I had arrived where I wanted to be. Home. I fell in love with the pristine beauty of this place and its people.

On Main Street all a person needs can be found—cards, wedding presents, pots and pans, even a pair of eyeglasses. The shopkeepers know your name. People greet one another on Main Street. Everyone belongs.

Town and gown thrive together. The diverse international community brings the world to Hanover, one that belies the idea of Hanover as a small town.

Volunteerism is a way of life here. An ethic of caring and a vibrant civic life shape the Upper Valley community. All of the organizations with which I have been associated, such as United Way and The Family Place, commonly strive to improve the health and wellbeing of the people in the region.

When I moved to Hanover the pioneering women of the Five College Book Sale welcomed me. Each spring we would take to the air promoting the sale on Rex Marshall's weekday morning radio program, "Breakfast at the Hanover Inn."

Little did I know what a community would come to mean to me when I developed breast cancer. If my difficult medical trial had to happen I am grateful it happened here. I felt the uncommonly kind embrace of the community. Friends encircled me while I was being treated at the Norris Cotton Cancer Center and the Hospital became a lifeline. Through this experience I realized the essence of community.

I have lived in Hanover Center, Etna, and Hanover for half my life. The love I felt from the first still endures.

— *Susan DeBevoise Wright (Jim and I live now in Sunapee. It's part of the Dartmouth-Lake Sunapee region but we consider Hanover home as well.)*

Susan DeBevoise Wright

During her career at Dartmouth that spanned more than three decades, Susan Wright held numerous positions involving service to students including associate director of Career Services, class dean for five undergraduate classes, advisor to international students, and honors coordinator for the Presidential Scholars and Mellon Minority Undergraduate Fellowship programs. These interests continued during the tenure of her husband, Jim Wright, as Dartmouth's president from 1998-2009, when she "was so much more than the President's wife" on campus while also being a volunteer for organizations that included Upper Valley United Way and the Norris Cotton Cancer Center.

Serving Youth and Seniors

Youth in Action

In January 1983, Maureen Hall gathered a handful of parents—Eileen Daschbach, Pam Whitfield, Barbara Hall and Joan Weider—to explore a program of community service for young people. Two months later, the group of moms invited 35 teens to a dinner, and the response was so enthusiastic that the program was immediately up and running.

Julie Appleton, Hanover High '83, suggested the name "Youth in Action" and Betsy Hall '86 designed the logo. Maureen Hall, the volunteer director, provided the skill and energy to organize the group into the ongoing service organization that remains very active today.

A series of projects grew quickly: the Getting to Know You Tea and Sing Along with Senior Citizens, a Get Acquainted barbecue for new students in the fall, the famous Applesauce Project, assistance with Special Olympics, and Christmas caroling.

Promoting, securing and nurturing support and financial help from organizations and individuals in the community were key to YIA's growth and success. By 1993, there were 150 students involved with the programs, assisted by 20 adult volunteers.

In 1994, the Town voted a small stipend to YIA and Kathy Geraghty was hired as a part-time director. Kathy served until 2006 when Jessica Eakin took over as YIA grew in student numbers and projects to assist a multitude of non-profit organizations. Chris Lord became the current director in 2010.

Today, YIA remains a vibrant organization that attracts the majority of high school students to participate in many activities. The organization adopted Bill Hammond's Pig and Wolf—they soon accompanied the students to many projects.

In 2013, YIA will celebrate its 30th birthday. Thanks to the vision of Maureen Hall, it remains a model of community service for schools through New Hampshire and Vermont.

The Senior Center

In 1975, when Hanover was applying for HUD funds to build a senior housing complex, a requirement of the HUD grant was that a meeting place be available for the tenants of the new apartments. Spurred by a committee made up of Dot Strong, Mary Major and Madlyn Munger, Hanover's Senior Center was born.

The activities at the center found its first home in the small Cape Cod-style home at 42 Lebanon St. The building soon became the home for the Senior Center as well as the Recreation Department, the Community Counselor, and Youth in Action. Seniors fondly remember Thanksgiving dinners in the old house, a variety of holiday parties, and daily drop-in activities—crafts, music and games.

Vicky Winters was the first paid part-time director. When Vicky was forced to retire for health reasons in 1990, Gail Schall took over.

In 2003, with the opening of the Richard Black Community Center and its new Senior Lounge, Gail's much-loved fitness programs have found room to expand. The senior center now bustles with a myriad of activities including luncheons, bridge games, fitness programs, painting—even a weekly movie. If seniors need help with computers, help is available, too.

Young and old now share in one of Hanover's most active community resources. *(W.B.)*

Members of Youth in Action serenade senior citizens with carols at the annual Christmas party.

Courtesy: Youth in Action

Connections

When your high school age children tell you to apply for a job, it catches your attention. I listened and was fortunate to be chosen to succeed founder Maureen Hall as the second director of Hanover's Youth in Action, a non-profit whose mission is to involve high school age young people in community service. I received this good news in typical Maureen fashion. She appeared at my door very early one morning carrying a symbolic "torch" to be passed on to me.

At that time, YIA had no place to call home and I didn't have room at my house to store all of the materials and unusual paraphernalia needed to run its projects and programs. Someone (I do not recall who) suggested that the old Senior Center on Lebanon Street across from Hanover High would make a fine place for the YIA director's "office." The building was a cozy old Hanover home with the offices for Gail Schall, Senior Center director, on the first floor and Dena Romero, the School and Community Counselor, on the second.

A meeting was set to determine what the impact of the arrival of YIA into the building might mean. The meeting went well: Gail and Dena were most welcoming. Further bonding evolved as Dena and I joined forces to battle with resident chipmunks and a devious muskrat that made it through the pipes to the little lavatory between our offices.

There followed years of supper forums, joint craft projects, teas, discussions, holiday parties, caroling and the famous fall Applesauce Project. One year a student from India became an avid YIA volunteer with a great affinity for working with the elderly. He came for the applesauce project. He helped pick the apples on Wednesday. On Thursday he washed the apples at the Senior Center. On Friday he spent hours slicing and peeling apples with a mix of generations. On Saturday morning he reappeared in the kitchen, took me aside and very solemnly asked, "Kathy, where is this sauce of which you speak?" By 4:30 that afternoon he had his answer and I sent him home with a quart container of the sweet, pink tinted sauce to share with his family.

The warm kitchen of the old Senior Center held so very many warm memories for those of us who volunteered with YIA during those years.

— *Kathy Geraghty*

During the Shrine parade in 1991, Youth in Action students ran a food café to benefit Hanover senior citizens.

Pig and Wolf

Editor's note: Pig and Wolf are central characters during Hanover's 250th celebration. Here's why—in the words of Willy Black, the chainsaw sculptor who created them.

One fall afternoon nine years ago, Bill Hammond, the Hanover High teacher who lives across Lebanon Street from the Hanover Co-op, called to ask a favor. "My wife collects pigs," he said. "Would you carve a wooden pig for her birthday?" Certainly, I replied, and the saga of Pig and, later, Wolf began.

The pig was carved and delivered in time for Christina's birthday on January 2, 2002. Bill stood the pig on their front porch, greeting all who drove by on Lebanon Street.

Soon, Bill began to dress the pig with a green sweater for St. Patrick's Day, then a bonnet with a basket full of eggs for Easter. Pig was taking on a life of her own. In the summer, she welcomed hikers on the Appalachian Trail, donning sunglasses to stop the summer glare. Pig advertised North Country Community Theater shows. Thanks to their inventive caretakers, Pig participated in many events.

The following year, I asked Bill if he wanted another pig so the two pigs could start a family. Bill said, "No, I want a wolf!" When Wolf arrived, he was a stealthy creature, never in plain view. Wolf spent several months creeping up to Pig. He peeked over the fence, hid behind the trees and in a pickup truck, reenacting the story of the Three Little Pigs. Bill secured a building permit and constructed each of the houses in his driveway. The drama played out during the summer.

Pig and Wolf took on a life of their own. Youth in Action students took them to community events. They were invited to children's birthday parties and changed costumes for events taking place in town.

When the Star Wars movie arrived at the Nugget, Pig and Wolf were dressed as Darth Vader and R2D2 and placed on the roof of the theater. After a week downtown, still in their Star Wars costumes, they ventured to the roof of the Hanover Co-op to greet drivers along Park Street.

Then, one morning, they disappeared, gone without a trace. The Valley News reported on their absence. Pig and Wolf had vanished. They were a hot topic of conversation.

Six months later, on a cold January morning, a driver coming south on I-91 outside of Norwich spotted the two on a hillside. Pig was lying peacefully on a barbecue grill. Wolf was toasting an imaginary marshmallow.

Pig and Wolf were back! Bill and Christine had a party with lawn ornaments to welcome them home. They happily resumed their lives as greeters and advertisers of happenings in town.

When the Hanover 250 Committee explored a community art project for the celebration, Pig and Wolf were selected as the featured subjects. Their "cousins" can be found around town this summer. The rest of the story is yet to be written. *(W.B.)*

Courtesy: Youth in Action

Pig and Wolf frequently have been dressed for special occasions by Youth in Action students. Here they're part of a Valentine's Day celebration.

Community Activity

Jerry Mitchell

When Dr. Bill Young joined the Hitchcock Clinic staff in 1976 he helped build a snow sculpture for Dartmouth's Winter Carnival. He's been a leading community volunteer, especially for the Dartmouth Winter Games and Occom Pond Party ever since. In 2011, Bill is co-chair with Julia Griffin for the Hanover 250 celebration.

Jon Gilbert Fox

Flying Squirrel Graphics

The Hanover Streetfest.

Since it opened in 2003, the Richard Black Community Center has become a hub of activity for Hanover's youth and seniors. Other photos on this page portray a range of special community events.

Flying Squirrel Graphics

The Occom Pond Party, successor to the Winter Games in recent years.

Flying Squirrel Graphics

Hanover's Old Fashioned Fourth of July Parade.

The Shrine Game and Parade

I had been working for the *Valley News* about four months in 1958. On a Friday afternoon, the managing editor said, "David, I want you to cover the Shriners in Hanover tomorrow. Jim (Wechsler) will do the football game. You cover the parade."

That was my introduction to what has become one of the premier sporting events in New England. The Shrine Maple Sugar Bowl has its roots in southern New Hampshire (Nashua, 1954 and Manchester, 1955-57), but the founding fathers knew that an all-star football game between New Hampshire and Vermont high school players could grow only if it was in a location central for both states.

The move to Hanover in 1958 was natural. Dartmouth was an enticing location because Memorial Field offered 13,000 seats. The 1958 game in Manchester had attracted only 5,000. The potential was easy to see.

Also, there were two local Shriners in Hanover who could pave the way—Forrie Branch, Hanover High School's football coach, and Sid Hazelton, Dartmouth's long-time swimming coach and a Hanover town official.

When I went to see my first Shrine Parade in Hanover that Saturday afternoon I could tell it was special. Main Street was crowded and there were people lined up along the Dartmouth Green, cheering every unit—the bands, the clowns, the funny vehicles. It was a scene that would be repeated 48 times.

My wife Ruth joined me in October 1959. In 1962, Linwood Bean, a Hanover businessman and general chairman of the Shrine Bowl, asked if I would write news releases for the game. I had moved to the alumni office at Dartmouth where I would work for 40 years. I enjoyed writing and saw an opportunity to repay a debt.

When Ruth was eight years old and living on a ranch in Colorado she was stricken with polio. Her mother had just passed away and her father was left with a family of six children. Ruth's father had heard of Shrine hospitals and their great work. After Ruth spent a year in a Colorado hospital, her father made the decision to move to Portland, Ore., the site of one the Shrine's 22 orthopedic hospitals. When Lin Bean asked, we both saw it as an opportunity to repay a debt of gratitude.

Shriners dressed as clowns riding their go-carts mesmerized children during the parade that made its way through downtown Hanover, preceding the Maple Sugar Shrine Game that was played at Dartmouth's Memorial Field from 1958 until 2007. Renovations to the field in 1967, 1968 and 2006 took the game from Hanover to other sites, as has been the case since 2008.

Over the next five years I would become a Mason and Shriner, joining Bektash Temple in 1967. Except for 1967, 1968 and 2006, when Memorial Field was being renovated, the Shrine parade and the Maple Sugar Bowl Game remained in Hanover until 2008 when the event moved as plans were unfolding for more renovations at Memorial Field. In 2011 the Shriners are exploring a permanent home for the parade and game—perhaps, again, in Hanover.

— *Dave Orr*

Trees and Gardens

Hanover citizens take both pleasure and pride in the flower gardens, the work of the Hanover Garden Club, that are found throughout the community. So, too, since 1978 the Town has received the Tree City USA Award, a national honor based on tree planning, funding, planting and preservation.

William Desch, the town arborist, and Mary Reynolds of the New Hampshire Division of Forests and Lands mark a tree planting that recognized Hanover as a Tree City USA honoree for the 30th time.

Courtesy: Town of Hanover

Courtesy: Town of Hanover

For decades, Nan King was the inspirational leader after the Hanover Garden Club. In 1960, the Garden Club took over management of numerous flower gardens that brighten the community.

Dartmouth College Library

Before Hanover had a Garden Club it had Julius Mason, a postman who lived on South Main Street and, starting in the 1930s, set out to plant flower gardens along his route. The bed of day lilies that Mason planted on South Main Street years ago continues to bloom each spring.

Joseph Mehling

Nearly 1,800 trees (about 75 different species, including this crabapple near Webster Cottage) make the campus of Dartmouth College one of the most beautiful in the nation. Since the 1960s, the Dartmouth Class of 1950's tree planting program has added more than 180 trees to the campus, earning it the title of The Tree Planting Class.

Jon Gilbert Fox

Throughout the summer, hanging planters are an added attraction along Main Street.

"Mass Transit"

Dealing with parking and the volume of private auto traffic that flows through Hanover is an ongoing issue.

In 1976, the Town initiated a shuttle bus service from the Thompson Arena parking lot that served the College and the hospital. In the ensuing six years the service was expanded to cover Lyme Road and the downtown areas. The bus service was financed by the Town's parking district and with contributions from the College and the Medical Center.

In 1984, with the demand for more parking and the growing need to accommodate regional commuters coming to town, Advance Transit became an independent New Hampshire non-profit corporation whose purpose was to offer transportation services to the Upper Valley community. Advance Transit is funded by a federal grant and contributions from participating towns in New Hampshire and Vermont, the College and the Medical Center.

In 1990, as the Medical Center prepared to move south to a new location just across the town line near Route 120, it was clear that a new shuttle service would be needed. In 1991 the new hospital opened and the Hanover Shuttle merged with Advance Transit.

In 1994 the Hanover Shuttle ceased operations. Funding from the Town and Dartmouth College was used to create a new Fare Free Zone along Advance Transit's Blue Route. From modest use at the outset, by 2000 the annual number of riders had increased to 289,000.

Today, there are nearly a half-million passenger trips per year on Advance Transit's fixed routes. Shuttle service at DHMC and in downtown Hanover carry an additional 350,000 passenger trips per year. This makes Advance Transit's ridership the second highest in New Hampshire, exceeded only by the University of New Hampshire's Wildcat Transit System.

Throughout the Upper Valley, AT's white and blue busses provide Hanover and the region with a valuable transportation resource. *(W.B.)*

Advance Transit busses have helped to reduce traffic congestion while aiding commuters in Hanover and throughout the Upper Valley.

Farmer's Market

"Buy local, eat local" is a fairly new mantra heard about the Upper Valley. For years there has been a Farmer's Market every Saturday morning in Norwich. Lebanon followed suit in the late 90s. The Hanover Chamber of Commerce picked up the ball in the summer of 2008, organizing a Farmer's Market in Hanover. The market opened on the top level of the municipal parking garage but, after successful negotiations with Dartmouth, the market moved to a corner of the Green in 2009.

The market operates on Wednesday afternoons. Sixty percent of the vendors sell food, fresh from the garden or kitchen, while the remaining 40 percent are local crafts people. Notable among the craft vendors is Hanover's own Dusty Coates with his wonderful burl bowls.

Dartmouth students crossing the Green are likely to buy a snack while the locals stock up on perishables and goodies for their families. The visitors can purchase locally grown beef, pork, and chicken, along with every tempting fruit and vegetable grown in the Upper Valley. A favorite dish for many is the homemade ice cream, made with local organic milk. *(W.B.)*

Since graduating from Hanover High in the mid-1980s, Dustin (Dusty) Coates, working from his home on Trescott Road, has become one of the region's leading artisans with his beautiful burl bowls.

The banner outside Town Hall announces Hanover weekly Farmer's Market.

Welcome Wagon

In 1982, my husband, Bob, began his tenure as dean of the Dartmouth Medical School. I supported our move from New Haven so the power and the pain caught me by surprise.

As a seasoned psychotherapist I was eager to explore the experiences of other women concerning relocation, and at this opportune time the late Betsy Magill telephoned. As a local "hostess" of Welcome Wagon, a national organization devoted to introducing newcomers to the services, facilities and goods offered by their communities, she proposed to visit me. In a heartbeat, I accepted.

Mrs. Magill—"call me Betsy"—was warm, friendly and knowledgeable. She liked to meet new people. She was intrigued by my wish to interview newcomers concerning their transitions and volunteered to ask those she visited for permission to give me their names. Soon I had a population of 42 women eager to tell their stories.

Betsy was the catalyst for a study that continued for two years. In bi-monthly interviews these women disclosed profound feelings of loss paralleling their positive new experiences: loss of home, loss of friends, loss of identity. I was entrusted with very private communications and protected their privacy with disguised names in my book that was published in 1990, The Trauma of Moving: Psychological Issues for Women.

In the book's foreword, Dartmouth Professor Elise Boulding raised a crucial question: How much planning does a town do for its newcomers?

Which raises another question: What is Hanover doing now?

— *Audrey T. McCollum*

Child Care

Over the past 50 years, with more and more women entering the work place, the face of child care has changed dramatically. In the 60s, most moms were "stay at home." The few who worked usually had their children cared for by a neighborhood friend. Today, many employers in the Upper Valley provide an in-house day care facility.

The Dartmouth College Child Care Center was the first facility opened to care for pre-schoolers, from infants to kindergarteners. DCC opened in rental space in the Ray School in 1984. In 1987, a new facility opened on Reservoir Road. Over the years there have been additions to the building. Today, Dartmouth Day Care serves over 80 children.

When it opened in 1991, Kendal provided day care for employees with pre-school children and offered service to local families with no Kendal affiliation. CRREL also joined the day care ranks in 1991, opening the Crayon and Cradle day care facility. All three of Hanover's day cares serve infants through school-age children.

Nursery schools have long been available for Hanover kiddies. The Hanover Nursery School opened its doors in 1932. The present facility off East Wheelock Street was constructed in 1956, accommodating the needs of up to 70 three-to-five year olds. Another nursery school that has been in business over the past four decades is the Hampshire Cooperative Nursery School. Originally housed in the White Church in Hanover, it now operates at the former Fullington Farm on Lyme Road. Nursery schools differ from day care since children only attend a half-day educational session.

These day care facilities and nursery schools are dedicated to challenging children to explore the world around them. Recognizing that young children "learn best by doing," local kids have been fortunate to be able to attend the facilities available to them. *(W.B.)*

Affordable Housing

The Hanover Affordable Housing Commission (HAHC) was established by action of the Select Board in 2001. The Commission's purpose is to develop and recommend to the Town permanently affordable housing policies and regulations. The Gile Hill development was shepherded by the HAHC through concept, design and into project management by Twin Pines Housing Trust and the Hartland Group. Gile Hill, when completed, will have 120 units. In 2011, 97 are finished—61 rentals and 36 condos. Of this total, 54 are affordable under government designation. Gile Hill was dedicated by Governor Lynch in October 2007. *(W.B.)*

The Gile Hill development near the Medical Center opened in 2007, Hanover's response to the need for affordable housing.

Both: Jon Gilbert Fox

The Philanthropists

White Mountain Insurance Group is the worldwide financial services holding company created by Jack Byrne about 20 years ago. Without fanfare, Byrne decided to locate White Mountain's corporate offices in Hanover.

With three sons who had graduated from Dartmouth in the 1980s, Byrne and his wife, Dorothy, were familiar with Hanover as an attractive place to work and live. And, as quietly as White Mountain has conducted business on South Main Street, Mr. and Mrs. Byrne have become Hanover's most generous philanthropists.

They established the Byrne Foundation to benefit a wide range of charitable organizations in Hanover, the Upper Valley and beyond. Mrs. Byrne is president of the foundation. Their sons (John III, Mark and Patrick) serve as directors.

The Byrne name is visible on a building at Tuck School and a Dartmouth residence hall. Their generosity has supported a professorship at Tuck, academic and student public service projects at Dartmouth, and the palliative care program at Dartmouth-Hitchcock Medical Center.

Less visible but no less valued in Hanover and the Upper Valley, the Byrne Foundation has supported non-profit initiatives too numerous to count.

Jack Byrne is now retired as chairman of White Mountain. Mrs. Byrne continues to oversee the generosity of the Byrne Foundation. As Mr. Byrne said in a newspaper profile several years ago, "I am in charge of receipts and Mrs. Byrne is in charge of disbursements. We make a good team. She has done a marvelous job." *(J.D.)*

Community of Faiths

While religious observance has been a constant in Hanover since the town's earliest days, there have been two notable additions to the community of faiths in the past 50 years, both on the Dartmouth College campus.

The College's Catholic students had been active through the Newman Club since 1924 but didn't have a permanent home until Aquinas House was built in the early 60s at the end of Webster Avenue. St. Clement's Chapel is the cornerstone, a three-building facility that includes McDonald Hall, a classroom and recreation building that connects the chapel to the chaplain's house.

A short distance away on Occom Ridge is the Roth Center for Jewish Life that opened in the late 90s. Dartmouth's first rabbi, appointed in 1975, served about 500 students and residents of the Upper Valley but it was a gift from an alumnus, Steven Roth, a Manhattan real estate developer, that made the building a reality as a community center for Dartmouth Hillel and the local Jewish community.

The churches serving other faiths in Hanover have also completed significant renovations in recent years, among them the Church of Christ at Dartmouth, St. Denis Church, St. Thomas Church and the Chapel of Our Saviour that respectively are home to the town's Protestant, Catholic, Episcopal and Lutheran communicants. *(J.D.)*

The Roth Center for Jewish Life on Occom Ridge opened in the late 1990s to serve the Jewish community at Dartmouth and surrounding communities.

David's House

To say that Hanover residents are generous is an understatement. As the first director of David's House, when it opened on Prospect Street near downtown Hanover in 1986, I learned first hand, over and over again, that Hanover folks care about others.

From the board of the Upper Valley Hostel, another Hanover non-profit that houses adults undergoing treatment at DHMC, the organizers of David's House obtained valuable information for establishing what has become a very successful non-profit with an overwhelming goal: to provide a home-away-from-home for families with sick children—with no start-up funds.

Tuck School offered expertise through a feasibility study that confirmed the reasons why this type of housing was necessary. Whenever there was a problem, there was someone to supply the answer: renovation—by Trumbull-Nelson's crew— of a large, old house that was sold to David's House by a Hanover property owner, even though it wasn't for sale; plumbing equipment —John Pope (F. W. Webb) and Dick Banker; interior decorating—Jeanie Stevenson and Isabel Farmer. Seemingly insurmountable problems worked themselves out with a lot of assistance from Hanover residents.

When David's House was ready to open, volunteers were needed. Numerous townspeople offered their time and energy to help make a warm, supportive atmosphere for families from all over the United States and beyond. Everything—from a gift of $100,000 to freshly baked cookies—were generously offered. It's what has made David's House so special from the beginning.

After DHMC moved to Lebanon in 1991 and the "new" David's House (twice as big as the original) opened in 1994, the support continued—and increased. Volunteers who were instrumental in the beginning are still a very important part of what makes David's House such a special place and starting out in Hanover certainly helped, along with the cookies. Over 10,000 families served by David's House over the past 25 years would agree. And, I'm sure those who guide the Upper Valley Hostel and Outreach House would, too.

— Jane DeGange, Executive Director of David's House, 1985-89, 1991-2005

There were seven guest bedrooms in the first David's House that opened on Prospect Street near downtown Hanover in the winter of 1985-86.

In 1994, three years after the Medical Center moved to Lebanon, the current David's House opened nearby with 15 guest bedrooms.

Both: Courtesy David's House

Kendal at Hanover

Kendal at Hanover, a continuing care retirement community, opened its doors to its first residents in July 1991. As an affiliate of Kendal Corporation in Philadelphia, Kendal at Hanover was founded by Quakers and is governed by the Quaker philosophy and values although the majority of its residents are not Quakers.

Until the 90s, many people thought retirement communities should be located in warm climates but Peter Bien, a Quaker and a Hanover resident, had another idea. He suggested to the Philadelphia group that Hanover needed a retirement community. The Hanover Meeting Group formed a planning committee. The rest is history, visibly at 80 Lyme Road.

Today Kendal at Hanover offers residents 250 different sized apartments, 56 skilled nursing beds, 38 assisted living units, and 18 special care units. The population at Kendal is about 500 residents. They have a wide spectrum of services and programs, and have completely put to rest the thought that retirement communities belong in the south! *(W.B.)*

Kendal at Hanover has grown since it opened in 1991. The continuing care retirement community on Lyme Road now has about 500 residents.

Both: Jon Gilbert Fox

Lyme Road

Fifty years ago, and for decades before that, land along Lyme Road was devoted to farming. Today, the farms have disappeared and the area about a mile north of downtown Hanover's newest village is a bustling cross-section of business and residential life as well as the site for the Town's public safety services and two public schools.

The Hanover Consumer Co-op's store at the corner of Lyme Road and Reservoir Road opened in 2009 and provides a "north of town" option for Co-op members and other shoppers who can also shop at Co-op locations near downtown Hanover, at Centerra Park in Lebanon, and, since 2010, in White River Junction, Vt.

To address traffic management north and south of the Richmond Middle School that opened in 2005, roundabouts were created on Lyme Road. The roundabouts were as much a conversation subject as the ornamental globes on Ledyard Bridge a decade earlier but, as with the globes, time has made them a part of the Hanover scene.

The business-professional building at 45 Lyme Road brought a new dimension of commerce to the area in the 1980s.

All: Jon Gilbert Fox

Golfside Farm

March 25, 1965: It was a controlled burn, a training exercise for the Hanover Fire Department. We could see the sadness in the eyes of my father, Earle, and my uncle, Raymond, as their family home became engulfed in flames, leaving only ashes and memories of the farm my grandparents bought in 1902.

After Ray's son, Bob (my cousin and close friend), decided that putting satellites in space (he became an engineer with Hughes Aerospace) was his calling, my uncle sold Golfside Farm to the College. Another of the proud and prosperous Lyme Road farms disappeared.

Golfside Farm was a dairy farm. As a child, I often accompanied my father on the milk route and had the opportunity to meet customers. Norris Cotton was one. Bette Davis, the actress, used to stop by the farm to visit my grandfather and pick up cream on the way to her home in Sugar Hill.

I grew up in the house across the street (next to the Lyme Road Co-op). My uncle and his family lived next door, where Hampshire House now stands. In the 1970s, that house was moved further north on Lyme Road.

This was a time when neighbors helped neighbors. Reservoir Road was a dirt road, so muddy in the spring that Dean Bob Strong needed to take one of the farm tractors to and from his home each day.

As the years passed, a snowy owl appeared frequently in the cupola of the deserted barn. The barn and the owl are now gone. The town rejected an offer of land for a school where the Curtis Road and Woodmore Drive development now stands, feeling it was "too far out of town."

Now, a middle school and an elementary school abut the former Garipay property. A day care is located on the old hayfield. Garipay Field is the home of Dartmouth's rugby teams. Reservoir Road has been reconstructed, complete with a sidewalk and streetlights. The Co-op sits where my grandfather's snack bar once stood. The old farm is now part of Hanover's newest "village." How times have changed in the past half-century!

— *Charlie Garipay*

The farmhouse that was home to the Garipay family for about 60 years before being sold to Dartmouth in the early 1960s, is consumed in a controlled burn on March 25, 1965.

Courtesy: Charlie Garipay

Today, the area that was once part of Golfside Farm is the site of Dartmouth rugby fields and Hanover recreation fields along Reservoir Road.

Jon Gilbert Fox

Farming in Hanover – Then and Now

All: Barrett Collection

End of an era: In 1971, Haslett Fullington, above left, and his brother, Wilson, the third generation of Fullingtons to operate the family farm, auctioned their herd of more than 240 cows that crossed Lyme Road from barn to pasture every day. It was Hanover's last working farm. Gone, too, were the Fullington's Dartmouth Dairy delivery trucks that served the Hanover community in the years after World War II.

All: Jon Gilbert Fox

In some respects it's a throwback, albeit on a smaller scale, to the 19th century when sheep outnumbered people in Hanover. At Muscle in Your Arm Farm in Etna, Lise and John Richardson keep a flock of sheep and llamas. The fleece from these animals is spun into yarn that is highly prized by knitters in the Upper Valley and beyond.

Hanover Center

Muster Day

In 1961, Lillian Bailey, a long-time resident of Hanover Center, and a much-loved teacher in the Hanover School system, conceived the idea for Muster Day, a ceremony held on May 30 at the entrance to the First Congregational Church of Hanover facing the Hanover Center Green and adjacent to the Hanover Center cemetery.

Each year, citizens gather in Hanover Center to honor our armed forces and those who have served, placing flags on graves in the nearby cemetery. Students in Lillian's third grade class memorized Lincoln's Gettysburg Address. Today, community children still recite Lincoln's address. Little did Lillian realize that she established a tradition that lives on. *(W.B.)*

Lillian Bailey (right) had the idea for Muster Day in Hanover Center as part of Hanover's bicentennial celebration in 1961. Muster Day has been celebrated ever since. Lillian is shown with Phoebe Storrs Stebbins whose ancestors were among Hanover's earliest settlers.

Nick Stone from Brattleboro, Vt., put his team of oxen through their paces at the Hanover Center Fair in 2008.

The Hanover Center Old Timers Fair is another June event that recalls the Town's history and traditions.

All: Jon Gilbert Fox

Mail boxes and road signs, official and unofficial, reflect the timeless rural nature that can still be found in Etna.

Hanover's first town library was incorporated in 1801 in Mill Village, as Etna was called in earlier days. This building, the Hanover Free Library, was completed in 1905 and cost $2,822.11 and continues, with Howe Library, to serve the community.

Tim Bent (right) has been tapping maple trees and boiling sap in Etna for 40 years. Glenn Elder (left), Tim's long-time friend and occasional helper for most of those years, is a member of a family that has lived in Etna for five generations. Glenn's son, Patrick, is the fifth generation of Elders to take part in this annual springtime enterprise.

The Etna Schoolhouse closed in 1957 and was falling into disrepair until Rick Dickinson, who has lived nearby for many years (members of his family had attended the school), bought and restored the building that is now Etna's post office.

The Sport for All Ages

The sports most closely associated with Dartmouth isn't football or hockey. It's skiing, the sport for a lifetime.

Ford Sayre learned to ski at Dartmouth. After graduating in 1933, he became manager of the Hanover Inn and developed, with his wife, Peggy, an accomplished skier, the Hanover Inn Ski School. Sayre died in a crash during a War Bond exhibition in 1944. Peggy and other local organizers established the Ford Sayre Memorial Ski School at Hanover Country Club and Oak Hill. In 1950, several children's skiing organizations merged their activities into the Ford K. Sayre Memorial Ski Council that continues to provide instruction programs at the Dartmouth Skiway and other sites.

These photos from the 1940s and 1950s reflect a time when equipment was simpler but enthusiasm for skiing was no less than it is today.

Political Scene

Perhaps more than in any town its size in New Hampshire, presidential campaigns are a happening in Hanover.

Over the years numerous candidates, Republican and Democrat, have come to Hanover to campaign and participate in nationally televised debates. Candidates of every stripe, riding the momentum of the day, have made political news in Hanover. Some highlights:

In 1963, before racial turmoil exploded in the southern states, Alabama governor George Wallace addressed a crowd of 3,900 in Leverone Field House. Four years later, on May 3, 1967, ex-Governor Wallace faced a raucous crowd of 1,400 Dartmouth students in Webster Hall. The turmoil tumbled outside and students started rocking Wallace's car. Hanover Police Chief Dennis Cooney called it "...the worst riot I've seen in 22 years." Dartmouth Dean Thad Seymour said, "(Wallace) picked up 100,000 votes last night."

On October 19, 1963, Nelson Rockefeller, a Dartmouth alumnus and governor of New York, stood outside Tanzi's Store and announced to a crowd, mostly Dartmouth's male students (nearly a decade before coeducation began) that clogged Main Street, his intention to seek the Republican nomination in 1964.

Rockefeller lost presidential bids to Barry Goldwater in 1964 and to Richard Nixon in 1968. He remained New York's governor until 1973. After Nixon resigned in 1974, President Gerald Ford nominated Rockefeller, under the 25th Amendment, to be vice president. That was as close as Rocky got to the Oval Office. He served under Ford until 1977 when he retired from politics.

In February 1976, the south-side seats of Thompson Arena were filled to hear California governor Ronald Reagan, making his first run at the presidency. Seats on the arena's north side were empty: Reagan's security people wouldn't permit anyone to sit behind him.

In 1984, Dartmouth's Rockefeller Center was jammed to the windowsills to hear John Glenn, the astronaut and senator.

The Hanover Inn, on May 6, 1987, was the setting for a bizarre media event. Senator Gary Hart from Colorado was an early frontrunner for the Democratic nomination in 1988 but he was coping with reports of an extramarital affair.

Hart dodged a barrage of pointed questions from the corps of national reporters that jammed the Heyward Lounge. When it was over and Hart headed north to Woodsville and Littleton, a reporter was asked, "This is a question of whether you believe him or not, right?"

"Yes," was the reply. The next question, "Do you believe him?"

"No," the reporter said, quietly shaking his head. The next morning in Littleton, with more damning news about to break, Hart said, "Let's go home." Later that day, in Denver, he ended his campaign.

Bill Clinton made numerous visits to Hanover, not including his visit as Dartmouth's commencement speaker in

Harry Tanzi, Hanover's honorary mayor, led the cheers in October 1963 as Nelson Rockefeller announced his intention to seek the Republican presidential nomination in 1964. Behind them is Rockefeller's wife, Happy.

Barrett Collection

1995 or when he came again in 2008 on behalf of his wife, Hillary Clinton.

In 2007, Barack Obama's rising popularity with young voters was captured in a large color photo in TIME Magazine as Obama spoke to students and local supporters packed in the wide walkway outside Rockefeller Center.

In many elections it appears that Hanover voted for the candidate rather than the party. There were alternate victories for Republican and Democratic candidates, not always reflecting the national choice.

In 1960, on the eve of Hanover's bicentennial in 1961, Republican Richard Nixon garnered 1,355 votes in Hanover compared to 848 for his Democratic opponent, John Kennedy, who narrowly won the national election.

By 2008, the town's registration profile had shifted dramatically (many Dartmouth students were now registered to vote in Hanover). John McCain, the Republican, had 1,328 votes in Hanover, slightly less than Nixon's 1960 supporters. In contrast, 6,140 supported Barack Obama (5,300 more than voted for JFK in 1960).

George McGovern won handily in Hanover in 1972, but lost to Nixon's national landslide. Jimmy Carter edged Ronald Reagan in 1980 (independent candidate John Anderson had almost a third of local votes) but Reagan won a substantial victory nationwide.

Over the years, Hanover has evolved from a Republican to a Democratic town, a trend reflected beyond national elections. For more than two decades, Democrats have dominated the town's delegation to the state legislature.

However, when it comes to voting for selectmen, Hanover voters have focused on the credentials of the candidates. Party affiliation isn't mentioned on the ballot. *(J.D.)*

Our Town

It happened when I was 18 years old. I filled out a form that asked for my hometown. Without thinking I wrote: "Hanover, N.H."

In truth, Hanover was not my hometown. My real hometowns have been on Boston's North Shore, in the national capital region and Pittsburgh. But from the day I stepped into Hanover, I regarded it as my hometown. Because in some elemental way I felt I had come home.

My uncle and my father had been members of Dartmouth's classes of 1941 and 1947, respectively. Throughout my childhood I had been steeped in Hanoveriana. I ingested the phrase "Hap and Hal's" even though I would never meet Hap nor Hal, nor ever visit that establishment. I had the vague sense that Tanzi's Market was an important step on the national political campaign trail, kind of a North Country version of the Sheraton Wayfarer, which I would come to visit innumerable times covering presidential politics. How was I supposed to know, at age 10, that only one presidential campaign was rooted there, and that that campaign (Nelson A. Rockefeller's) ended poorly? It was a matter of conviction in my family that the only decent breakfast north of Salem, Mass., was served at Lou's. It is still true, by the way. Five members of my family have sworn to it.

Thus it was incontrovertible that Hanover was my home, sort of in a Robert Frost kind of way. It was our own RF, as my beloved friend Edward Connery Lathem would call him, who wrote that the land was ours before we were the land's, and so Hanover was mine before I was, strictly speaking, Hanover's.

The thing about Hanover, or at least about my Hanover, was how it possessed me, almost certainly because it had so many possessives. Ward's Department Store and Serry's Clothiers and Tailors both had that telling apostrophe that made you know that someone from around here was in the back room and took pride in what was in the front window. Then there was Lou's, and I knew Lou Bressett. There was Campion's, and I knew a few Campions and at least one James Campion. There was Peter Christian's, and I knew Peter's father, Murray Washburn. There was Pat and Tony's, and I knew both Pippins. There was Ward Amidon's, and I knew him, too. And of course there was Duke's Framing & Art Supplies on Allen Street, and I knew the estimable Alfred Duclos, who distributed grays and wisdom from the depths of Davis Varsity House (to almost every freshman football player, "You're not big enough to play at Dartmouth...go down to Harvard.") and his brother, Richard, equally a legend. Times may have changed, however, and not for the better. I am not sure how many of today's students have ever known a Dirt Cowboy.

Then there was the Dartmouth Bookstore. I have a tiny, framed picture of it in my office, right behind me as I type this now. Of course I knew Wil Goodhue, the manager in my day, but the person who made me know I could be at home in those beguiling stacks was one of his assistants, David Marks. That's because my name is David Marks Shribman.

But David and Lou and the Campions and the Pippins and Doc Greenan over at Dartmouth Printing (the brother of Nola Catabriga, the secretary in the office where I learned at the hands of the indispensible Jack DeGange) and don't forget the Dukes were as much a part of my Dartmouth education and experience as any course I took. In later years I would come to know seven presidents. I am prouder to have known Jim Campion and Lou and the brothers Duke. By and large they were better company.

David Shribman was Dartmouth's Class Day speaker in 1976.

All of these people—and every block of this place—remain giant presences in my memory. I do not remember where I had lunch yesterday. I remember every lunch I ever had at the Green Lantern with George F. Theriault, mentor to two Shribmans in two generations. I remember sitting with a pretty girl on the steps leading down to Peter Christian's. I remember wondering how Tommy Keane managed to procure the softest gray T-shirts in America for the Indian Shop, later the Big Green Shop, at the adjacent location, and I would trade my car for one of them now.

I remember seeing John Sloan Dickey at football practice, James O. Freedman in the bookstore, James Wright holding hands with his lovely Susan at the Inn corner, and my daughter has witnessed the latest of the Jims, President Kim, at a Main Street restaurant. Did Alan Jay Lerner go to Dartmouth? I am asking because in our town, you walk down the street on the chance that you meet, and you meet not merely by chance.

One last story about why I love my hometown, and it involves someone I met not merely by chance. But of a summer's evening in 1974 I was walking down East Wheelock toward Valley Road when I encountered the redoubtable Judge Amos Blandin, who knew that inside I burned to be a newspaperman, back when that meant something. "David," he asked, "have you re-read Allison Danzig's account (in *The New York Times*) of the 1965 Dartmouth-Princeton game lately?" I hadn't, of course. But I re-read it that night, and, after recalling this story, I re-read it again tonight. Worth it, too.

Now back to RF. That remark about the land being ours comes from one of his best-loved poems. Frost recited it from memory at John F. Kennedy's inauguration exactly a half-century before this writing. It is not a coincidence that the poem's title is The Gift Outright. To me, and to tens of thousands of others, Hanover was The Gift Outright. It's time so many of us recognized that, and said thanks. It was your hometown, not ours, but you were generous enough to share it. I loved it then. I think I love it even more now.

— David M. Shribman, Dartmouth '76 and a College trustee from 1993-2003, won a Pulitzer Prize in 1995 for his national political coverage. He is executive editor of the Pittsburgh Post-Gazette.

Writers

This is the last piece to be written for this book. Consider it a thank you note from the editor to the many people who have contributed perspectives that tell stories about Hanover in recent years.

Writing is easy. Good writing is hard. For some of the contributors, their pieces were good—and easy. For others, it was hard work but they came out well, too.

Contributors to this book are, for the most part, amateur writers. Hanover has had its share of notable residents who write for money: Jodi Picoult, Janet Evanovich, Bill Bryson and Willem Lange come to mind. Also, Corey Ford.

David Shribman, my friend for the past 40 years, lived in Hanover only as a Dartmouth student but still considers it his hometown. His contribution appears at the end of the book because the editor opted to save the best for last.

Hanover was Corey Ford's hometown from 1952 until his death in 1969. Ford published 30 books and more than 500 magazine articles with a gregarious sense of humor. Many reflected his love for dogs including an article, *My Dog Likes It Here*, about life in Hanover that includes these thoughts:

"My dog made up my mind to live in Hanover. My dog is a large English setter, who acquired me when he was about six months old. A good dog-town is a friendly town. Hanover is like that. Which is why my bird dog would rather live here in Hanover than any other place in the world. I'm glad that he decided as he did. I feel the same way."

So do I, even though, after living in Hanover for 21 years, Jane (my wife and *my* editor) and I have lived down the road in Lebanon for the past 20 years. But, like David Shribman, we still consider Hanover our hometown.

— Jack DeGange

Adrian Bouchard

Corey Ford with Tober, son of Cider, the English setter that prompted Ford to move to Hanover in 1952.

Appendix

Facts About Hanover

Incorporated: 1761

Location: Grafton County, N.H.

Geographic Coordinates: 43°42'08"N, 72°17'22"W

Government: Board of Selectmen, Town Manager

Area: 50.2 square miles includes 49.1 square miles of land, 1.2 square miles of water
Elevation: 528 feet

Highest point: North peak of Moose Mountain (2,313 feet)

Population: 10,850 in 2000, 11,000 (estimate) in 2010 (Population includes Dartmouth College students)

Hanover is bordered by the towns of Lyme, Canaan and Enfield, N.H., the City of Lebanon, N.H., and the town of Norwich, Vt.

Inside the limits of Hanover are the rural villages of Etna and Hanover Center.

Sister Cities: Joigny, France (1993); Nihonmatsu, Japan (1998)

Public Schools: The Dresden School District, the first interstate school district in the United States (1963), includes Hanover High School, the Frances C. Richmond Middle School, and the Bernice A. Ray Elementary School in Hanover, and the Marion Cross Elementary School in Norwich, Vt.

Town Managers

Neil Berlin, 1967-74

John (Jack) Stinson, 1975-78

Peter Gartland, 1978-83

Clifford Vermilya, 1983-96

Julia Griffin, 1996 to present

As town manager from 1983-96, Cliff Vermilya guided Hanover's town government into the computer age and provided an effective leadership voice during the relocation of the Dartmouth-Hitchcock Medical Center.

Town of Hanover

Village Precinct Commissioners

1961 - Fletcher Low, Lewis Bressett, John Neale, Kenneth LeClair, Niles Lacoss, Robert McLaughry
1962 - Fletcher Low, Lewis Bressett, John Neale, Kenneth LeClair, Niles Lacoss, Robert McLaughry
1963 - Niles Lacoss, Lewis Bressett, Fletcher Low, Kenneth LeClair, Donald Cameron, Robert McLaughry

Board of Selectmen
(* = Chair)

1964 - Lewis Bressett*, Donald Cameron, Kenneth LeClair, Robert McLaughry, David Nutt
1965 - Lewis Bressett*, David J. Bradley, Donald Cameron, Kenneth LeClair, David Nutt
1966 - Lewis Bressett*, David J. Bradley, Edward Brown, Robert McLaughry, David Nutt
1967 - David Nutt*, David J. Bradley, Edward Brown, Donald Cutter, Robert McLaughry
1968 - David Nutt*, Edward Brown, William Crooker, Donald Cutter, Robert McLaughry
1969 - David Nutt*, Edward Brown, William Crooker, Donald Cutter, John Milne

1970 - David Nutt*, Edward Brown, William Crooker, Donald Cutter, John Milne
1971 - David Nutt*, Edward Brown, Donald Cutter, Donald Hawthorne, John Milne
1972 - David Nutt*, Edward Brown, Donald Cutter, Donald Hawthorne, John Milne
1973 - Edward Brown*, Harry Bird, Edgar Mead, John Milne, John Skewes
1974 - Edward Brown*, Donald Hawthorne, James Campion III, Edgar Mead, John Skewes
1975 - James Campion III*, Donald Hawthorne, Martha Solow, Edgar Mead, John Skewes
1976 - James Campion III*, Donald Hawthorne, Martha Solow, Stephen Waite, Roy Banwell
1977 - James Campion III*, Martha Solow, Stephen Waite, Roy Banwell, Benjamin Thompson
1978 - James Campion III*, Martha Solow, Stephen Waite, Roy Banwell, Benjamin Thompson
1979 - James Campion III*, Martha Solow, Stephen Waite, Sharon Nordgren, Benjamin Thompson

1980 - James Campion III*, Martha Solow, Stephen Waite, Sharon Nordgren, Benjamin Thompson
1981 - James Campion III*, Stephen Waite, Sharon Nordgren, Benjamin Thompson, Marilyn Black
1982 - James Campion III*#, Sharon Nordgren*, Thomas Byrne%, Benjamin Thompson, Stephen Waite, Marilyn Black
    (# = Died, October 1982; % = Appointed to complete James Campion's term)
1983 - Sharon Nordgren*, Warren Craumer, Marilyn Black, Stephen Waite, Benjamin Thompson
1984 - Sharon Nordgren*, Stephen Waite, Marilyn Black, Jack Nelson, Benjamin Thompson
1985 - Sharon Nordgren*, Stephen Waite, Marilyn Black, Jack Nelson, Benjamin Thompson
1986 - Sharon Nordgren*, Stephen Waite, Marilyn Black, Jack Nelson, Robert Kirk
1987 - Sharon Nordgren*, David Cioffi, Robert Kirk, Marilyn Black, Jack Nelson
1988 - Robert Kirk*, Marilyn Black, Jack Nelson, David Cioffi, Katherine Connolly
1989 - Robert Kirk*, Marilyn Black, Jack Nelson, David Cioffi, Katherine Connolly

1990 - Robert Kirk*, Marilyn Black, Katherine Connolly, Murray Washburn, Jack Nelson
1991 - Robert Kirk*, Marilyn Black, Murray Washburn#, George Gamble, Katherine Connolly, Jack Nelson%
    (# = Resigned, July 1991; % = Completed Washburn's term)
1992 - Marilyn Black*, Jack Nelson, Katherine Connolly, George Gamble, Dorothy Behlen Heinrichs
1993 - Marilyn Black*, Jack Nelson, Katherine Connolly, George Gamble, Dorothy Behlen Heinrichs
1994 - Marilyn Black*, Jack Nelson, Dorothy King, Katherine Connolly, Dorothy Behlen Heinrichs
1995 - Marilyn Black*, Katherine Connolly, Dorothy King, Jack Nelson, Dorothy Behlen Heinrichs
1996 - Marilyn Black*, Jack Nelson, Katherine Connolly, Dorothy King, Brian Walsh
1997 - Marilyn Black*, Jack Nelson, Katherine Connolly, Brian Walsh, John Manchester
1998 - Marilyn Black*, Katherine Connolly, Brian Walsh, John Manchester, John Colligan
1999 - Brian Walsh*, Marilyn Black, Katherine Connolly, John Manchester, John Colligan

2000 - Brian Walsh*, Katherine Connolly, Marilyn Black, William Baschnagel, Judson Pierson
2001 - Brian Walsh*, Katherine Connolly, Marilyn Black, William Baschnagel, Judson Pierson
2002 - Brian Walsh*, Katherine Connolly, William Baschnagel, Peter Christie, Judson Pierson
2003 - Brian Walsh*, Katherine Connolly, Peter Christie, William Baschnagel, Judson Pierson
2004 - Brian Walsh*, Katherine Connolly, William Baschnagel, Peter Christie, Allegra Lubrano
2005 - Brian Walsh*, Katherine Connolly, William Baschnagel, Peter Christie, Allegra Lubrano
2006 - Brian Walsh*, Katherine Connolly, William Bacschnagel, Peter Christie, Allegra Lubrano
2007 - Brian Walsh*, Katherine Connolly, William Baschnagel, Peter Christie, Athos Rassias
2008 - Brian Walsh*, Katherine Connolly, William Baschnagel, Peter Christie, Athos Rassias
2009 - Brian Walsh*, Katherine Connolly, Peter Christie, Athos Rassias, Judy Doherty
2010 - Brian Walsh*, Katherine Connolly, Peter Christie, Athos Rassias, Judy Doherty
2011 - Brian Walsh*, Katherine Connolly, Peter Christie, Athos Rassias, Judy Doherty

Index

Notes:

(1) Photographs, illustrations, and associated captions are indicated by bold page numbers.

(2) Nicknames are indicated in parentheses following the formal name.

(3) Information in the chronology headers is indicated by italicized page numbers.

Index

Index

Index

Index

Index

Index

Index

Index

TOWN *of* HANOVER
1761-2011